Austria Travel Guide 2025

Explore Vienna, Salzburg, Hallstatt, and the Alps with Itineraries, Local Tips, and Hidden Gems

BY

MARKO OLIVER

1

Marko Oliver

2

DISCLAIMER NOTICE

This travel guide is intended for informational purposes only. While every effort has been made to ensure the accuracy and reliability of the information provided at the time of publication, the author and publisher make no representations or warranties regarding the completeness, currentness, or suitability of the content. Travel regulations, business hours, prices, and conditions may change without notice.

Readers are encouraged to verify details independently and consult official sources before making travel plans. The author and publisher disclaim any liability for loss, damage, or inconvenience caused as a result of reliance on this guide.

TABLE OF CONTENTS

4

5

6

9

10

11

13

14

Introduction
Welcome to Austria

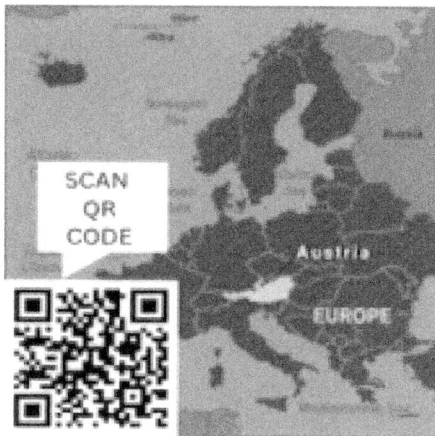

Austria is a country where nature, culture, and history converge to create a travel experience unlike any other. Situated in the heart of Europe and bordered by eight countries, Austria offers a diverse blend of landscapes, from snow-covered alpine peaks to gentle river valleys, from grand imperial cities to serene lakeside villages.

This nation boasts a remarkable legacy. For centuries, Austria was at the center of European politics and culture, shaped by the powerful Habsburg dynasty. The result is a country steeped in grandeur—evident in the palaces of Vienna, the baroque architecture of Salzburg, and the Gothic cathedrals scattered throughout the countryside. Yet Austria is far more than a repository of history. It is a modern, innovative country that celebrates the arts,

15

embraces sustainability, and offers some of the most efficient infrastructure in Europe.

Travelers are drawn here not only for the architectural splendor and classical music but also for the outdoor activities. Austria's Alps are a world-class destination for skiing, snowboarding, hiking, and cycling. The Danube River weaves through romantic towns and wine-growing regions, perfect for leisurely cruises and gourmet experiences. And then there's Hallstatt—one of the most picturesque villages in the world, nestled beside a serene lake with dramatic mountain backdrops.

Austria in 2025 is more accessible and welcoming than ever. With updated tourism services, expanded eco-tourism options, and a renewed emphasis on regional traditions and cultural heritage, now is the perfect time to visit. This guide will introduce you to the highlights and hidden gems, providing insights that go beyond surface-level recommendations. You'll not only know what to visit, but understand the meaning and history behind it—enriching your travel experience with context and connection.

Whether you're visiting for five days or five weeks, Austria offers endless possibilities. This book aims to help you navigate them with ease and excitement.

Who This Guide is For

Austria appeals to a broad range of travelers. This book is written specifically with readers from the **United States**,

United Kingdom, and **other European countries** in mind, but the advice is applicable to any international traveler seeking a thoughtful, enriching experience.

First-Time Visitors

If you're traveling to Austria for the first time, this guide will give you everything you need to feel confident and prepared. You'll learn how to get around, what to expect at restaurants and hotels, how to use public transportation, and which cities or towns best match your interests. We also provide a cultural primer to help you avoid common misunderstandings and navigate everyday situations with ease.

From airport arrivals and currency exchange to tipping customs and holiday schedules, the basics are covered so you can focus on enjoying your trip.

Experienced European Travelers

If you've already explored other parts of Europe—France, Germany, Italy, or Switzerland—you may think you know what to expect in Austria. However, this country has its own personality and set of traditions. Austrians take pride in regional identity, which can vary dramatically from one province to the next.

This guide helps experienced travelers go deeper: you'll discover which wine regions are emerging in 2025, why the Viennese coffeehouse is considered a cultural institution, and how local festivals reveal Austria's deeply rooted customs. We also offer advice on traveling by train, renting a car, or taking scenic routes that lead you off the beaten path.

Outdoor Enthusiasts

Austria is a haven for nature lovers. In winter, the Alps offer some of the best skiing and snowboarding in Europe. In summer, the mountains transform into a playground for hikers, climbers, cyclists, and paragliders. Lakes such as Wolfgangsee and Achensee attract swimmers, kayakers, and paddleboarders.

This guide highlights Austria's best outdoor adventures by region and season. You'll find information about equipment rentals, guided tours, safety regulations, and eco-friendly practices. Whether you're a seasoned athlete or a casual explorer, you'll discover the perfect destination to match your skill level and interests.

Culture and History Enthusiasts

Austria is a cultural powerhouse. It was the birthplace or adopted home of historical figures like Mozart, Beethoven, Freud, and Gustav Klimt. Its cities are filled with opera houses, museums, concert halls, and libraries that showcase the country's profound influence on European thought and creativity.

This guide caters to history buffs and culture seekers by highlighting lesser-known sites, offering walking tours of historic neighborhoods, and exploring the stories behind

18

monuments and artwork. We also include current exhibitions, festivals, and cultural events happening throughout 2025.

Culinary Travelers

Austria's cuisine is hearty, flavorful, and deeply regional. From Viennese schnitzel and apple strudel to alpine cheeses and Styrian pumpkin seed oil, food is an essential part of the Austrian experience. And it's not just about eating—it's about where and how you eat. The traditional Austrian *Gasthaus*, the refined Viennese café, and the rustic mountain hut all offer distinct atmospheres.

This guide explores food by region and season. You'll find recommendations for local specialties, farmers' markets, wine tastings, and food festivals. We also include tips on where to dine well on a budget and how to enjoy authentic meals outside of tourist zones.

Families, Seniors, and Inclusive Travelers

Austria is ideal for travelers of all ages and abilities. Its excellent infrastructure makes it easy to get around, and public safety is consistently ranked among the highest in Europe. Whether you're a family with young children, an older couple looking for comfort and accessibility, or a traveler with mobility needs, this guide has you covered.

You'll find suggestions for family-friendly attractions, slower-paced itineraries, barrier-free accommodations, and medical services. We also provide advice on navigating

19

cities with strollers, choosing accessible transportation, and staying connected while traveling.

How to Use This Book

This guidebook is designed to be both comprehensive and easy to navigate. Whether you're planning your trip months in advance or searching for ideas on the go, you can use this book in a way that fits your travel style.

Chapter Layout

The book is divided into 15 detailed chapters, each focused on a city, region, or theme. These chapters provide historical context, must-see attractions, suggested itineraries, and travel tips. Chapters are designed to stand alone, so you can jump directly to the section most relevant to your current plans.

For example:

- If you're spending three days in Vienna, head to the Vienna chapter for top sights, dining, transportation, and suggested walking tours.

- If you're interested in hiking in the Alps, skip to the chapter on Alpine Adventures.

- If you're planning a culinary tour, check out the Austrian Cuisine chapter.

20

Each chapter includes:

- Featured highlights

- Historical and cultural context

- Practical information (hours, prices, transportation)

- Local recommendations

- Travel safety and etiquette notes

Icons and Visual Elements

Rather than relying on maps and illustrations (which may be available in the companion PDF or website), this book uses clear subheadings, bullet points, and consistent formatting to make information easy to find. Important details—like costs, addresses, or reservation advice—are presented in clean, scannable sections.

We avoid overwhelming the reader with too much text in one section. Instead, we use short paragraphs, side notes, and clear formatting to enhance readability.

Travel Planning Tools

In the appendix, you'll find several printable and digital-friendly tools:

21

- A customizable budget planner

- Sample itineraries for 3, 7, 10, and 14-day trips

- Daily travel journal pages

- Restaurant and experience logs

- Packing checklists for all seasons

These resources are designed to help you stay organized and maximize your time while minimizing stress.

On-the-Go Usability

The content is structured to be useful during your trip—not just before. If you're navigating a new city or adjusting your plans due to weather or timing, you can use this guide to quickly look up nearby attractions, dining options, or public transit tips.

Where possible, we provide alternate options, such as indoor activities for rainy days or quieter alternatives to crowded landmarks.

Cultural and Sustainable Travel Focus

This guide encourages thoughtful, responsible travel. We include:

22

- Guidance on how to engage respectfully with locals

- Information on sustainability efforts and eco-conscious accommodations

- Tips for minimizing environmental impact

- Suggestions for supporting small, local businesses

We also highlight opportunities for deeper engagement—such as visiting open-air museums, attending regional festivals, or taking a cooking class led by local chefs.

23

Chapter 1
Austria at a Glance

Geography and Climate

Austria is a landlocked country in Central Europe, bordered by Germany, the Czech Republic, Slovakia, Hungary, Slovenia, Italy, Switzerland, and Liechtenstein. With a total area of approximately **83,879 square kilometers (32,386 square miles)**, Austria may be modest in size, but its diverse geography offers striking contrasts and immense beauty.

Geographic Regions

Austria is generally divided into five major geographical regions:

1. **The Eastern Alps** – Covering around 62% of the country, this region dominates western and central Austria. It includes some of the most iconic mountain ranges such as the Tyrolean Alps, the Hohe Tauern (where Grossglockner, Austria's highest peak at 3,798 meters, is located), and the Dachstein massif.

2. **The Alpine Foreland and Foothills** – These hilly areas transition between the mountainous west and the flatter east, and are home to picturesque towns,

24

vineyards, and scenic lakes.

3. **The Pannonian Plain** – Found in eastern Austria, particularly around Vienna and Burgenland, this region has a warmer, drier climate and fertile soil, ideal for agriculture and wine production.

4. **The Danube Valley** – The Danube River flows for over 350 km through Austria, shaping valleys, towns, and trade routes. Important cities like Vienna, Linz, and Krems lie along its course.

5. **The Bohemian Forest and Granite Plateau** – Located in the north, especially in Upper Austria and parts of Lower Austria, this region features forested highlands and ancient rock formations.

Climate Overview

Austria experiences a **temperate continental climate**, with four distinct seasons:

- **Spring (March–May):** Mild temperatures, blooming meadows, and gradually increasing daylight. A great time for sightseeing and hiking.

- **Summer (June–August):** Warm and occasionally hot, especially in the east. Temperatures range from 25°C to 35°C (77°F to 95°F). This is the peak season for outdoor activities like mountain biking, lake swimming, and alpine trekking.

25

- **Autumn (September–November):** Crisp air, golden forests, and grape harvests in wine regions. Temperatures range from 10°C to 20°C (50°F to 68°F).

- **Winter (December–February):** Cold and snowy in mountainous regions, making it perfect for skiing and snowboarding. Cities may experience snow and frost, with temperatures often dropping below freezing.

Each region has its own microclimate, and travelers are advised to pack appropriately based on their itinerary.

A Brief History

Austria's history is deeply intertwined with the political and cultural evolution of Europe. Its journey from a medieval duchy to a Habsburg empire, and eventually to a modern republic, reflects the shifting tides of power, religion, war, and peace.

Early Settlements and Roman Influence

The area now known as Austria was originally settled by Celtic tribes. By the 1st century BCE, it was absorbed into the Roman Empire as part of the provinces of Noricum and Pannonia. Roman roads, towns, and military posts laid the groundwork for future urban development.

26

The Rise of the Babenbergs and the Habsburg Dynasty

In the 10th century, Austria became part of the Holy Roman Empire. The Babenberg dynasty ruled until the 13th century, when the powerful **Habsburg family** took over. From 1278 onward, the Habsburgs turned Austria into the center of a sprawling European empire.

By the 16th century, the Habsburgs controlled not only Austria, but also Hungary, Bohemia, parts of Italy, and eventually Spain and its colonies. Vienna became a political and cultural hub, especially during the Renaissance and Baroque periods.

Austro-Hungarian Empire

In 1867, Austria united with Hungary to form the **Austro-Hungarian Empire**, one of the largest and most diverse political entities in Europe. Its influence stretched across the Balkans and Central Europe, fostering developments in architecture, music, science, and philosophy.

However, the empire was not immune to rising nationalism and social unrest. It ultimately collapsed following World War I, leading to the birth of the **First Austrian Republic** in 1918.

20th Century and World Wars

27

Austria's interwar years were marked by economic hardship and political instability. In 1938, Austria was annexed by Nazi Germany in an event known as the **Anschluss**. It remained part of Nazi rule until the end of World War II in 1945.

After the war, Austria was divided into occupation zones but regained independence in 1955, declaring **perpetual neutrality**, which remains a cornerstone of its foreign policy today.

Modern Austria

Austria joined the European Union in 1995 and adopted the euro in 2002. It has since maintained a reputation for political neutrality, strong public infrastructure, and a high standard of living. Today, Austria balances its imperial heritage with a forward-looking commitment to sustainability, innovation, and cultural preservation.

Languages and People

Official Language

The official language of Austria is **German**, specifically the Austrian variant known as *Österreichisches Deutsch*. While standard German is taught in schools and used in media and official documents, regional dialects (especially in Tyrol, Vorarlberg, and Styria) can differ considerably from textbook German.

28

Most Austrians are multilingual, particularly in urban areas. English is widely spoken in hotels, restaurants, shops, and tourist attractions—especially in Vienna, Salzburg, and major ski resorts.

Other Recognized Languages

Austria also recognizes several minority languages in specific regions:

- **Slovene** in southern Carinthia

- **Croatian and Hungarian** in Burgenland

- **Czech and Slovak** in Vienna

These linguistic rights reflect the country's multicultural past and legal protections for ethnic minorities.

Cultural Traits

Austrians are often described as:

- **Polite and reserved** – formal greetings (like "Grüß Gott" or "Guten Tag") are the norm.

- **Punctual and orderly** – being late is frowned upon.

29

- **Proud of tradition** – festivals, folk music, and regional dress are celebrated throughout the year.

Family life, environmental stewardship, and quality of life are all core values. Austrians enjoy a high level of education, universal healthcare, and public services.

Currency and Time Zone

Currency

Austria is a member of the **Eurozone**. The official currency is the **Euro (€)**.

- **Coins** come in denominations of €0.01 to €2

- **Banknotes** include €5, €10, €20, €50, €100, €200, and €500 (though the €500 is rarely used in daily transactions)

Credit and debit cards (especially Visa and Mastercard) are widely accepted, but some smaller establishments—especially in rural areas—may prefer cash. ATMs (locally called *Bankomaten*) are widely available.

Time Zone

Austria is in the **Central European Time Zone (CET)**:

30

- **Standard time**: UTC +1

- **Daylight Saving Time (DST)**: UTC +2 (from the last Sunday in March to the last Sunday in October)

Travelers from the United States and United Kingdom should be aware of the time difference:

- **New York to Vienna**: +6 hours

- **London to Vienna**: +1 hour

Most public transportation, appointments, and event listings follow a **24-hour clock**, so 3:00 PM is written as 15:00.

Why Visit Austria in 2025?

Austria in 2025 is a destination that combines timeless charm with modern innovation. Here are several compelling reasons to make it your next travel destination:

1. Cultural Highlights and Special Events

- **Vienna Philharmonic's 2025 Jubilee**: One of the world's most prestigious orchestras is celebrating a major anniversary with a year-long concert series and special events across Austria.

- **UNESCO Anniversary in Salzburg**: Celebrating Salzburg's designation as a World Heritage Site,

31

the city will host exhibitions on Mozart, architecture, and medieval trade.

- **Contemporary Art Focus**: Austria's museums and galleries are spotlighting contemporary Austrian artists in exhibitions running throughout 2025, especially in Graz and Linz.

2. Sustainable Travel Upgrades

Austria continues to lead in **green tourism**. In 2025:

- National parks have improved trail systems with digital navigation.

- Many hotels now operate with 100% renewable energy.

- Eco-pass discounts are available on train travel and museum entries for tourists who arrive by rail or bike.

3. Culinary Renaissance

The **2025 Culinary Heritage Campaign** is highlighting traditional regional foods with a modern twist. Enjoy:

- Organic farm-to-table dishes in Styria

- Vegan versions of Austrian classics like schnitzel and goulash

- Wine tasting routes with local vintners in Burgenland and Lower Austria

4. Easy Accessibility

Austria's commitment to tourism infrastructure is stronger than ever. In 2025:

- Rail routes are faster and more frequent, with new panoramic trains connecting Salzburg to Zell am See and Hallstatt.

- Contactless payment systems are standard across public transport.

- Multilingual signage has been expanded, especially in rural and alpine destinations.

5. Year-Round Attractions

Whether you're skiing in Kitzbühel, hiking through Hohe Tauern National Park, or enjoying a spring coffee in Vienna's Schönbrunn Gardens, Austria is a 12-month destination. Festivals, wellness spas, scenic drives, and romantic old towns offer experiences suited to every season.

Austria at a glance offers more than just practical information—it provides context for your journey. From its majestic geography and fascinating history to its modern achievements and cultural depth, Austria in 2025

33

is ready to welcome curious and conscientious travelers
from around the world.

Chapter 2
Planning Your Trip

Planning a successful trip to Austria in 2025 starts with thoughtful preparation. This chapter covers the best times to visit based on weather and festivals, visa information for different nationalities, budgeting tips for various types of travelers, must-have travel insurance, and a detailed packing checklist to suit every season.

Best Times to Visit

Austria is a year-round destination, but when you should go depends on your interests—whether it's skiing, hiking, cultural events, or relaxing by alpine lakes.

Spring (March to May)

Pros:

- Nature bursts into bloom, especially in parks, meadows, and the Wachau Valley.

- Fewer tourists, making it ideal for city sightseeing and countryside exploration.

- Mild temperatures and increasing daylight.

Events:

35

- Easter markets in Vienna and Salzburg.

- Tulip festivals and wine tastings in Lower Austria.

Average Temperatures:

- Vienna: 8–18°C (46–64°F)

- Salzburg: 6–17°C (43–63°F)

Recommended Activities:

- Walking tours

- Wine region visits

- Museum-hopping

Summer (June to August)

Pros:

- Long, sunny days with warm temperatures.

- Peak time for hiking, biking, and swimming in alpine lakes.

- Lively open-air events, especially classical music and film festivals.

Events:

- Salzburg Festival (opera, theatre, music)

- Vienna Film Festival

- Donauinselfest in Vienna (Europe's largest free open-air music festival)

Average Temperatures:

- Vienna: 20–30°C (68–86°F)

- Innsbruck: 18–28°C (64–82°F)

Recommended Activities:

- High-altitude hiking

- Lake activities in Carinthia

- Outdoor concerts

Autumn (September to November)

Pros:

- Fewer crowds and lower prices after summer.

- Colorful foliage and grape harvests in wine regions.

- Cool but comfortable weather.

37

Events:

- Wine harvest festivals (especially in Burgenland and Styria)

- Viennale (Vienna International Film Festival)

Average Temperatures:

- Vienna: 10–20°C (50–68°F)

- Graz: 8–18°C (46–64°F)

Recommended Activities:

- Vineyard tours

- Forest hikes

- Cultural events

Winter (December to February)

Pros:

- Austria is a winter sports paradise.

- Magical Christmas markets and snow-covered villages.

- World-class ski resorts and thermal spas.

38

Events:

- Christmas markets across Austria

- Vienna New Year's Concert

- Ski World Cup events in Kitzbühel and Schladming

Average Temperatures:

- Vienna: -1 to 4°C (30–39°F)

- Tyrol Alps: -5 to 2°C (23–36°F)

Recommended Activities:

- Skiing, snowboarding, sledding

- Spa and wellness retreats

- Holiday shopping

If you're after **culture and sightseeing**, spring and autumn are ideal. For **outdoor adventures**, opt for summer or winter, depending on your preference for hiking or skiing.

39

Visa and Entry Requirements

Entry requirements vary depending on your nationality and the length of your stay. Austria is a **Schengen Area** country, so Schengen visa rules apply.

For U.S., U.K., and E.U. Citizens

United States:

- No visa required for tourism stays up to 90 days within a 180-day period.

- **ETIAS (European Travel Information and Authorization System)**: Starting in **mid-2025**, U.S. travelers will need to apply for ETIAS online before entering Austria.

United Kingdom:

- Post-Brexit, U.K. citizens can travel to Austria visa-free for up to 90 days in a 180-day period.

- ETIAS will also apply to U.K. travelers starting in 2025.

European Union Citizens:

- Free movement. No visa or travel authorization required.

- Valid national ID or passport suffices.

40

ETIAS at a Glance (Effective 2025):

- Cost: €7 per adult (free for under 18s and over 70s).

- Valid for 3 years or until your passport expires.

- Apply online with passport, email, and a debit/credit card.

- Approval is typically immediate but can take up to 4 days.

Other Requirements

- Passport must be valid for **at least 3 months beyond your intended departure** from Austria.

- Must have proof of return or onward travel.

- Travel insurance with medical coverage is highly recommended (and required for Schengen visa holders).

Schengen Visa (Non-Visa-Exempt Travelers)

Travelers from countries that do not qualify for visa-free entry must apply for a Schengen visa via an Austrian consulate or embassy.

Documents typically required:

41

- Completed application form

- Passport photos

- Proof of accommodation

- Travel itinerary

- Proof of financial means

- Valid travel insurance

Processing Time: Around 15 working days.

Budgeting Your Trip

Austria can be affordable for backpackers and luxurious for splurgers. Your budget will depend on the cities you visit, the season, and your travel style.

Daily Budget Estimates (Per Person)

Budget Type	Accommodation	Food & Drink	Transport	Activities	Total/day
Budget	€25–€50	€10–€20	€5–€10	€10–€15	€50–€90
Mid-range	€60–€120	€20–€40	€10–€20	€15–€30	€105–€210
Luxury	€150+	€50+	€25+	€30+	€255+

42

Money-Saving Tips

- **City Cards:** Vienna and Salzburg offer passes with free public transit and museum entry.

- **Public Transport:** Trains and buses are reliable and affordable. Regional passes are available.

- **Lunch Menus:** Many restaurants offer discounted **Mittagsmenü** (lunch specials).

- **Water:** Tap water is safe and excellent—bring a refillable bottle.

- **Grocery Stores:** Great for fresh, cheap meals and snacks (try Billa, Spar, or Hofer).

Example 7-Day Itinerary Budget (Mid-Range Traveler)

- 2 nights in Vienna: €300 (hotel + meals + activities)

- 2 nights in Salzburg: €250

- 2 nights in Innsbruck: €250

- Transport (rail and local): €100

43

- Misc. expenses: €50
  Total: €950–€1,000 per person

Travel Insurance

Travel insurance is essential—not only for peace of mind but also because it's required for travelers needing a Schengen visa.

Why You Need It

- Covers **trip cancellations, medical emergencies, baggage loss, and delays.**

- Essential for winter travelers engaging in **skiing or snowboarding.**

- Many healthcare providers abroad will require proof of insurance or upfront payment.

What to Look For

- **Emergency medical coverage:** Minimum €30,000 (as required by Schengen regulations).

- **Trip cancellation & interruption**

- **Lost or delayed baggage**

44

- **Winter sports or high-risk activity add-ons** (if applicable)

- **24/7 emergency assistance**

Packing Checklist for Austria

Packing for Austria requires a thoughtful approach, especially due to its changing seasons and terrain.

General Packing List

- Valid passport + photocopies

- Travel insurance documents

- Visa/ETIAS confirmation (if applicable)

- Credit/debit cards and some cash in Euros

- Universal power adapter (Type F sockets; 230V)

- Travel guidebook or offline maps

- Refillable water bottle

- Daypack or small travel backpack

- Language phrasebook or translation app

45

Clothing by Season

Spring & Autumn:

- Light sweater or fleece

- Waterproof jacket

- Long pants/jeans

- Scarf and gloves (for cooler mornings/evenings)

- Comfortable walking shoes

Summer:

- T-shirts and shorts

- Sunglasses and sunhat

- Light jacket (for mountain regions)

- Swimwear

- Hiking sandals or sturdy shoes

Winter:

- Thermal layers

- Insulated winter jacket

46

- Hat, scarf, gloves

- Waterproof boots

- Ski/snow gear (if applicable)

Extras for Outdoor Activities

- Hiking boots

- Trekking poles

- Reusable shopping bag

- Travel towel

- Sunscreen and insect repellent

- Ski goggles and snow gloves (for winter sports)

Health & Hygiene

- Prescriptions + doctor's note

- Basic first-aid kit

- Reusable face mask (still required in some areas)

- Hand sanitizer

47

- Toiletries (most items are available in Austrian stores)

Austria offers an unforgettable experience, and good planning is key to making the most of it. Whether you're scaling alpine peaks, sipping wine in the Wachau Valley, or enjoying a concert in Vienna, knowing what to expect helps make your journey smooth, safe, and memorable.

48

Chapter 3
Vienna – Imperial Elegance & Urban Culture

Vienna Austria Capital

Austria's capital, Vienna, is a mesmerizing fusion of imperial grandeur, artistic brilliance, and cosmopolitan charm. Once the heart of the Austro-Hungarian Empire, this city remains a cultural powerhouse, blending Baroque architecture with a thriving contemporary scene. From royal palaces and historic cafés to world-class museums and classical concerts, Vienna offers something for every traveler.

In this chapter, we'll explore Vienna's top attractions, hidden gems, and vibrant neighborhoods. You'll also find

49

tips on where to stay, where to eat, and how to take unforgettable day trips—all essential for planning a remarkable visit to Austria's most iconic city.

Top Attractions: Schönbrunn Palace, St. Stephen's Cathedral

Schönbrunn Palace

Schönbrunn Palace

One of Europe's most magnificent Baroque residences, **Schönbrunn Palace** was the summer residence of the Habsburg dynasty. With 1,441 rooms, lush gardens, and grand architecture, it offers a stunning glimpse into imperial life.

Highlights:

50

- **Grand Tour (40 rooms)**: Includes the opulent Great Gallery and the private apartments of Emperor Franz Joseph and Empress Elisabeth (Sisi).

- **Gardens and Gloriette**: Stroll through manicured lawns, fountains, and hedge mazes, and climb to the Gloriette for panoramic city views.

- **Schönbrunn Zoo**: The oldest zoo in the world, perfect for families.

- **Palmenhaus (Palm House)**: A giant greenhouse filled with exotic plants.

Practical Info:

- **Address:** Schönbrunner Schloßstraße 47, 1130 Vienna

- **Opening Hours:** Daily, 8:30 AM – 5:30 PM (extended in summer)

- **Entry Fee:** €22–€29 for tours; garden access is free

51

St. Stephen's Cathedral (Stephansdom)

St. Stephen's Cathedral (Stephansdom)

In the heart of Vienna's historic center stands St. Stephen's Cathedral, a Gothic masterpiece that's been the spiritual symbol of Austria for over 700 years.

Highlights:

- **South Tower (Steffl):** Climb 343 steps for a breathtaking view of Vienna.

- **Catacombs Tour:** Explore the eerie underground crypts.

- **Pummerin Bell:** One of the largest bells in Europe, housed in the North Tower.

52

- **Mosaic Roof:** Admire the iconic colorful tiles from the outside and above.

Practical Info:

- **Address:** Stephansplatz 3, 1010 Vienna

- **Opening Hours:** Daily, 6 AM – 10 PM (tours available until early evening)

- **Entry Fee:** Free to enter; tower and catacomb tours €6–€16

Museum Quarter and Historic Cafés

MuseumQuartier (MQ)

MuseumQuartier

53

One of the largest cultural complexes in the world, **MuseumQuartier** (MQ) is a creative hub housing everything from classical art to cutting-edge design.

Must-Visit Museums:

- **Leopold Museum:** Home to works by Egon Schiele and Gustav Klimt.

- **MUMOK:** Vienna's Museum of Modern Art, featuring contemporary and experimental pieces.

- **Kunsthalle Wien:** Focuses on current trends and interdisciplinary exhibits.

- **ZOOM Children's Museum:** Interactive learning for kids.

Things to Do:

- Relax in the courtyard lounges with coffee or cocktails.

- Explore design stores and art installations.

- Join public workshops or film screenings.

Opening Hours: Vary by museum; most open 10 AM – 6 PM (closed Mondays)

Address: Museumsplatz 1, 1070 Vienna

54

Vienna's Historic Coffeehouse Culture

Declared part of UNESCO's intangible cultural heritage, Vienna's **traditional coffeehouses** are institutions where time slows down, and intellectual debate once thrived.

Top Historic Cafés to Visit:

- **Café Central:** Frequented by Trotsky and Freud, this 19th-century gem offers chandeliers, piano music, and delicious cakes.

- **Café Sacher:** Home of the original Sachertorte (chocolate cake with apricot jam).

- **Café Demel:** An imperial confectioner with ornate interiors and glass-walled pastry kitchens.

- **Café Landtmann:** Sigmund Freud's favorite; ideal for people-watching near the University.

What to Order:

- **Melange:** Similar to a cappuccino, made with espresso and steamed milk.

- **Apfelstrudel:** Traditional apple strudel with whipped cream.

- **Sachertorte:** A decadent chocolate cake with a hint of apricot.

55

Vienna's Classical Music Scene

Vienna is the **City of Music**, having nurtured legends like Mozart, Beethoven, Haydn, and Strauss. Today, classical music thrives in opulent concert halls and intimate venues across the city.

Top Venues to Experience Classical Music

- **Wiener Staatsoper (Vienna State Opera):**

    - One of the world's top opera houses, with over 300 performances a year.

    - **Tip:** Get standing-room tickets for under €15 if booked early.

- **Musikverein:**

    - Home of the Vienna Philharmonic Orchestra.

    - The **Golden Hall** is considered one of the finest concert halls globally.

    - **Don't Miss:** The famous **New Year's Concert** (tickets by lottery or broadcast live).

- **Konzerthaus:**

56

- ○ Hosts both classical and contemporary performances.

- ○ Features jazz and international artists as well.

- **Haus der Musik:**

  - ○ An interactive sound museum celebrating Austria's music history and the science of sound.

Where to Hear Mozart

- **Concerts in Baroque venues** like **Karlskirche (St. Charles Church)** and **Palais Schönborn** offer candlelit Mozart performances by costumed musicians.

Day Trips from Vienna

Thanks to excellent rail and road connections, Vienna is the perfect base for fascinating day trips.

1. Wachau Valley and Melk Abbey

- A UNESCO World Heritage Site along the Danube, dotted with vineyards, medieval towns, and baroque churches.

57

- **Top Stops:**

  - **Dürnstein:** Charming town with castle ruins and wine tastings.

  - **Melk Abbey:** A lavish Benedictine abbey with golden libraries and hilltop views.

- **Getting There:** 1–1.5 hours by train or car. Danube boat cruises are available in warmer months.

2. Bratislava, Slovakia

- **Just 1 hour away** by train or boat, Bratislava makes for a quick international getaway.

- **Highlights:**

  - Old Town's cobbled streets and pastel buildings.

  - Bratislava Castle with panoramic views of the Danube.

  - Cafés and pubs with great value.

3. Vienna Woods (Wienerwald)

- Hike or cycle through forested hills just outside the city.

58

- **Heiligenkreuz Abbey** and **Mayerling** offer historical interest.

- Ideal for picnics and nature walks.

4. Baden bei Wien

- A spa town 40 minutes from Vienna known for its thermal baths and rose gardens.

- **Tip:** Visit the Beethoven House and enjoy wine tasting in local Heurigen (wine taverns).

Where to Stay and Eat in Vienna

Best Neighborhoods to Stay

Area	Vibe	Ideal For
Innere Stadt (1st District)	Historic, upscale	First-timers, sightseeing
Leopoldstadt (2nd District)	Riverside, family-friendly	Parks, Prater, families
Neubau (7th District)	Trendy, artsy	Hip cafés, boutiques
Margareten (5th District)	Local charm, budget-friendly	Budget travelers, longer stays

Recommended Hotels

Luxury:

- **Hotel Sacher Vienna** – Historic 5-star hotel next to the Opera House.

- **The Ritz-Carlton Vienna** – Elegant with a rooftop terrace and spa.

Mid-Range:

- **Hotel Das Tigra** – Comfortable, centrally located.

- **25hours Hotel at MuseumsQuartier** – Funky, eclectic design with city views.

Budget:

- **Wombat's City Hostel** – Popular with backpackers, clean and sociable.

- **MEININGER Hotel Downtown Franz** – Stylish and affordable.

Where to Eat: From Traditional to Trendy

Traditional Austrian Cuisine:

- **Plachutta Wollzeile:** Famous for **Tafelspitz** (boiled beef in broth).

60

- **Figlmüller:** Home of Vienna's most iconic (and oversized) **Wiener Schnitzel**.

- **Gasthaus Pöschl:** A cozy tavern serving local favorites.

Trendy and Modern:

- **Steirereck:** A 2-Michelin-star Restaurant known for modern Austrian dishes using local ingredients.

- **Labstelle:** Farm-to-table fine dining in a chic setting.

Street Food and Markets:

- **Naschmarkt:** Vienna's most famous market for international eats, fresh produce, and local delicacies.

- Try **Käsekrainer** (cheese-filled sausages) from Würstelstände (Sausage stands).

Vegetarian/Vegan:

- **Swing Kitchen:** Vegan burgers and fast food.

- **Tian Bistro:** Upscale vegetarian with a creative menu.

61

Insider Tips for Visiting Vienna

- **Vienna City Card:** Offers free public transport and discounts on major attractions.

- **Public Transport:** Reliable and extensive. Use the U-Bahn, trams, and buses. Buy 24, 48, or 72-hour tickets.

- **Free Sundays:** Some museums offer free entry on the first Sunday of the month.

- **Water Fountains:** Vienna has drinkable water fountains throughout the city.

- **Tipping:** Round up or leave 5–10% in restaurants.

Vienna is a city where imperial history and artistic innovation coexist beautifully. Whether you're wandering palace grounds, sipping a Melange in a chandelier-lit café, or losing yourself in Mozart's melodies, every corner of Vienna whispers elegance. With world-class museums, vibrant neighborhoods, and easy access to scenic day trips, it's no surprise that Vienna consistently ranks as one of the world's most livable—and lovable—cities.

62

Chapter 4
Salzburg – Mozart's City of Music and Charm

Salzburg view

Nestled on the banks of the Salzach River and framed by the majestic Alps, Salzburg is one of Austria's most enchanting cities. Renowned worldwide as the birthplace of Wolfgang Amadeus Mozart, Salzburg exudes a rich musical heritage combined with stunning Baroque architecture and a vibrant cultural scene. Its charming Old Town, impressive fortress, and lively festivals create an unforgettable atmosphere that draws visitors year-round.

63

In this chapter, we'll explore Salzburg's historical heart, dive into the city's deep connection with music, discover the best ways to experience its iconic Sound of Music legacy, sample local markets and cuisine, and recommend ideal places to stay.

Historic Old Town and Fortress Hohensalzburg

Salzburg's Old Town (Altstadt)

Salzburg's Old Town (Altstadt)

Salzburg's Old Town is a UNESCO World Heritage site, celebrated for its impeccably preserved Baroque architecture, narrow cobbled streets, and vibrant squares. It's the perfect place to wander on foot, soaking in the atmosphere of centuries-old churches, palaces, and quaint shops.

Key Highlights:

- **Getreidegasse:** This famous shopping street is lined with wrought-iron guild signs, boutique

64

shops, and Mozart's birthplace at No. 9. Visit the Mozart Museum to learn about his early life.

- **Residenzplatz:** A grand square with the Salzburg Residenz palace, once home to archbishops, and surrounded by impressive fountains.

- **Mozartplatz:** Dominated by the statue of Mozart, this square is an homage to the composer's legacy.

- **Salzburg Cathedral (Dom):** A Baroque masterpiece with a stunning facade and a richly decorated interior. Its crypt and baptismal font are especially significant in Mozart history.

- **St. Peter's Abbey:** One of the oldest monasteries in the German-speaking world, featuring beautiful catacombs and a historic cemetery.

Fortress Hohensalzburg

Fortress Hohensalzburg view

65

Dominating the skyline since 1077, the **Festung Hohensalzburg** is one of Europe's largest and best-preserved medieval fortresses. Perched atop the Festungsberg hill, it offers spectacular panoramic views of the city and Alps.

What to Explore:

- **State Rooms:** Lavishly furnished rooms showcase medieval weapons, armor, and artwork.

- **Golden Hall and Chapel:** Ornate chambers with intricate frescoes.

- **Marionette Museum:** Fascinating puppetry collection that reflects Salzburg's theatrical traditions.

- **Funicular Railway:** A convenient ride up to the fortress adds to the experience.

Practical Info:

- **Opening Hours:** Daily, 9 AM – 5:30 PM (seasonal changes apply)

- **Entry Fee:** Approx. €12 for adults; combined tickets with museums available

- **Tip:** Visit early morning or late afternoon to avoid crowds.

Sound of Music Tour

Salzburg is synonymous with **The Sound of Music**, the beloved 1965 film that brought the city's scenic beauty and Austrian culture to the world's attention. For many visitors, retracing the steps of the von Trapp family is a highlight.

Top Stops on the Sound of Music Tour:

- **Mirabell Gardens:** Featured in the famous "Do-Re-Mi" song sequence with its floral patterns and Pegasus Fountain.

- **Leopoldskron Palace:** The iconic lakeside villa used for exterior shots of the von Trapp family home.

- **Hellbrunn Palace:** The gazebo featured in the "Sixteen Going on Seventeen" scene.

- **St. Gilgen and Wolfgangsee:** Nearby picturesque towns and lakes where parts of the movie were filmed.

- **Nonnberg Abbey:** The real-life abbey where Maria was a novice.

Taking the Tour:

67

- Numerous operators offer guided bus tours ranging from 3 to 5 hours.

- Self-guided options with maps and audio guides are also popular.

- Some tours include visits to the Salzburg Sound of Music Museum.

Tips for Fans:

- Book tours in advance, especially during summer and festival season.

- Combine the Sound of Music tour with a visit to Salzburg's historical sites for a full experience.

Salzburg Festival and Music Heritage

Salzburg Festival

The **Salzburg Festival** is one of the world's most prestigious music and drama festivals, held every summer since 1920. It celebrates classical music, opera, and theater, attracting international performers and audiences.

Festival Highlights:

- Performances at the **Felsenreitschule**, **Großes Festspielhaus**, and **Mozarteum**.

- Legendary productions of Mozart's operas and dramatic plays.

- Outdoor concerts in scenic settings.

When to Visit:

- Late July to August is festival season—book tickets months in advance.

- If you miss the festival, smaller concerts and events run year-round.

Other Musical Attractions

- **Mozarteum University:** A world-renowned music conservatory with concerts open to the public.

- **Haus für Mozart:** A modern concert hall dedicated to Mozart's works.

- **St. Sebastian's Church:** Known for excellent acoustics and classical music performances.

- **Mozart Dinner Concerts:** Combine dining with live Mozart-era music in elegant venues.

Local Markets and Cuisine

Salzburg's Markets

Salzburg boasts lively markets that are perfect for sampling local flavors and crafts.

- **Salzburger Christkindlmarkt (Christmas Market):** One of the most atmospheric Christmas markets in Europe with festive lights, mulled wine, and handcrafted gifts.

- **Schranne Market:** A daily farmers' market with fresh regional produce, cheese, and baked goods.

- **Augustiner Bräu Keller Market:** Combines traditional beer garden atmosphere with local foods on weekends.

- **Green Market (Grünmarkt):** Open-air market for fresh fruits, vegetables, flowers, and snacks.

Typical Salzburg Cuisine

Salzburg's culinary traditions blend hearty Alpine flavors with refined Austrian classics.

- **Kasnocken:** Cheese dumplings similar to macaroni and cheese.

- **Salzburger Nockerl:** A light, sweet soufflé dessert, iconic to Salzburg.

- **Steirisches Wurzelfleisch:** Slow-cooked pork with root vegetables.

70

- **Mozartkugel:** Chocolate and marzipan pralines named after Mozart, a must-buy souvenir.

- **Traditional Taverns (Gasthäuser):** Enjoy Wiener Schnitzel, roasted meats, and seasonal game.

Best Accommodations

Salzburg offers a wide range of accommodations, from luxury hotels to charming guesthouses and budget hostels.

Luxury Hotels

- **Hotel Sacher Salzburg:** Elegant riverside hotel with a rich history and the famous Sacher Torte.

- **Hotel Goldener Hirsch:** Located in the Old Town, combining tradition with modern comfort.

- **Sheraton Grand Salzburg:** Modern luxury with spa facilities near the Mirabell Gardens.

Mid-Range Options

- **Hotel am Mirabellplatz:** Comfortable, central location near major attractions.

- **Boutique Hotel Auersperg:** Stylish hotel close to the fortress and river.

- **Star Inn Hotel Salzburg Zentrum:** Affordable, clean, and well connected.

Budget Stays

- **Yoho International Youth Hostel:** Popular with backpackers, friendly atmosphere.

- **MEININGER Hotel Salzburg City Center:** Convenient and value-focused.

- **Pension Adlerhof:** Cozy guesthouse with excellent reviews for value and service.

Insider Tips for Visiting Salzburg

- **Walking City:** Salzburg's compact size means most attractions are walkable; wear comfortable shoes.

- **Public Transport:** Buses cover outlying areas well; consider the Salzburg Card for free entry and transport.

- **Early Booking:** Especially in festival season and holidays, book accommodations and tours well in advance.

- **Weather:** Summers are mild, but pack layers for cooler evenings; winters bring snow, perfect for

72

festive markets.

- **Photography:** Sunrise and sunset provide magical light for capturing the fortress and river scenes.

Salzburg's combination of history, music, and Alpine charm makes it an essential stop on any Austrian itinerary. Whether you're exploring the Baroque streets of the Old Town, enjoying a performance at the Salzburg Festival, or following the footsteps of the von Trapp family, the city offers a magical experience that resonates with visitors long after they leave. Its unique blend of culture and natural beauty makes Salzburg a true jewel of Austria's travel landscape.

Chapter 5

Hallstatt – Fairytale Village on the Lake

Hallstatt view

Hallstatt is often described as a fairytale come to life — a tiny village nestled between towering mountains and the serene waters of Lake Hallstatt. Its postcard-perfect setting, rich history, and tranquil atmosphere have made it one of Austria's most beloved destinations. The village's charming streets, traditional Alpine houses, and stunning natural surroundings offer a uniquely peaceful yet inspiring experience.

74

This chapter will guide you through Hallstatt's iconic lakeside views, the fascinating salt mine and dramatic Skywalk, boat tours and nature trails, the best photography spots, and practical advice on whether to visit as a day trip or stay overnight.

Iconic Lakeside Views

Hallstatt's most defining feature is its breathtaking location on the western shore of Lake Hallstatt (Hallstätter See). The combination of crystal-clear lake waters, quaint wooden houses, and steep mountain cliffs creates an almost surreal landscape.

The Village Waterfront

The lakeside promenade is the heart of Hallstatt. Here, you'll find:

- **Colorful Alpine Houses:** Traditional multi-story homes with flower-filled balconies line the shore.

- **Boat Docks:** Small fishing boats and passenger ferries bob gently, inviting exploration.

- **Local Cafés and Restaurants:** Many offer lakeside terraces perfect for soaking in views while sipping coffee or enjoying fresh fish dishes.

75

Lake Hallstatt

Lake Hallstatt view

Spanning about 8 kilometers in length, Lake Hallstatt is part of the larger Salzkammergut region's network of lakes. Its clear waters reflect the surrounding mountains, creating mirror-like vistas.

- **Swimming and Relaxation**: In summer, designated swimming areas attract visitors who want to cool off.

- **Fishing**: The lake is home to trout and other freshwater fish.

- **Peaceful Ambiance**: Early morning or late evening are ideal times to enjoy the lake's calmness, often with mist hovering above the water.

76

Hallstatt Salt Mine and Skywalk

Hallstatt Salt Mine (Salzwelten Hallstatt)

Hallstatt Salt Mine view

Hallstatt's history is closely linked to salt mining, which dates back over 7,000 years, making it one of the world's oldest salt mines. Visiting the salt mine offers a fascinating glimpse into this ancient industry.

What to Expect:

- **Guided Tours:** Explore tunnels, wooden mining carts, and ancient tools. Tours include a thrilling slide used by miners.

- **Exhibits:** Learn about salt's role in Hallstatt's economy and its impact on European trade routes.

- **Salt Lake:** A hidden underground lake inside the mine, adding an element of wonder.

Visitor Tips:

77

- Book tickets online ahead of time during peak seasons.

- The mine is family-friendly but involves walking and some uneven surfaces.

- Wear sturdy shoes and bring a light jacket as the mine temperature is cool year-round (~8°C).

Hallstatt Skywalk "Welterbeblick"

For sweeping views of the village, lake, and surrounding mountains, the Hallstatt Skywalk is a must-visit.

- **Location:** About a 15-minute uphill walk from the village center or accessible by shuttle.

- **The Platform:** Extends 360 meters above the valley, offering panoramic vistas of the Dachstein mountains and Lake Hallstatt.

- **Sunrise and Sunset:** Particularly stunning times to visit, with vibrant colors lighting up the landscape.

Practical Info:

- The skywalk is open year-round but check local schedules.

- There is a small entrance fee, often included with salt mine tickets.

78

- Accessible by foot or shuttle bus for those less able to hike.

Boat Tours and Nature Trails

Boat Tours on Lake Hallstatt

A boat tour is one of the best ways to appreciate Hallstatt's beauty from a new perspective. Several options are available:

- **Electric Boat Rentals:** Rent a small electric boat to explore the lake independently, perfect for couples or families.

- **Guided Ferry Tours:** Ferries connect Hallstatt with other villages like Obertraun, offering scenic trips with commentary on local history and nature.

- **Photography Cruises:** Some tours focus on sunrise or sunset cruises, ideal for photographers.

Tips for Boat Tours:

- Check the ferry schedule, especially outside peak season when service is limited.

- Bring waterproof gear and sunscreen, as the weather can change quickly on the lake.

- Consider combining a boat tour with a visit to the salt mine or skywalk for a full-day experience.

Nature Trails and Hiking

Hallstatt is surrounded by dramatic Alpine landscapes, making it a gateway to excellent hiking and nature walks.

Popular Trails:

- **Echerntal Valley Trail:** A gentle walk along the valley with waterfalls and forest scenery, suitable for families.

- **Five Fingers Trail:** A challenging hike leading to a spectacular cliffside viewing platform shaped like five fingers, overlooking the Dachstein Glacier.

- **Dachstein Krippenstein Plateau:** Offers various trails with stunning views, alpine flora, and opportunities for mountain biking.

Hiking Tips:

- Trails range from easy to strenuous; choose based on your fitness level and time.

- Wear appropriate footwear and carry water and snacks.

- Early mornings are quieter and cooler for hiking.

80

Photography Spots

Hallstatt is a photographer's dream with endless opportunities to capture idyllic Alpine beauty.

Must-Visit Photography Locations

- **View from the Opposite Shore:** The best panoramic shots of Hallstatt's waterfront and village are taken from across the lake, especially at sunrise.

- **Market Square (Marktplatz):** Picturesque square with the iconic church spire and colorful houses.

- **Catholic Parish Church and Ossuary:** Known for its unique bone house decorated with painted skulls, providing hauntingly beautiful photos.

- **Salt Mine Entrance and Slide:** Action shots and architectural details.

- **Skywalk Platform:** Captures dramatic vistas and lake reflections.

- **Fishing Boats and Wooden Docks:** Great for close-up details of village life.

- **Snowy Winter Scenes:** Hallstatt in winter is magical, with snow-covered rooftops and frozen lake sections.

81

Photography Tips

- Visit early or late in the day to catch golden hour lighting.

- Use a tripod for low light or sunset shots.

- Explore off the beaten path for less crowded views.

- Respect private property and avoid trespassing on private docks or gardens.

Tips for Day Trips vs. Overnight Stays

Day Trips to Hallstatt

Many visitors come to Hallstatt as a day trip from Salzburg or Vienna, thanks to its relative proximity and efficient transport links.

Advantages:

- Convenient and easy to fit into a larger Austrian itinerary.

- Quick glimpse of the village, lake, and main attractions.

- Less expensive as you don't need accommodation.

Considerations:

- Can feel rushed, especially during peak tourist seasons.

- Crowds can be heavier mid-day, reducing the peaceful ambiance.

- Limited time for hikes or boat tours.

Overnight Stays in Hallstatt

Spending a night or two in Hallstatt offers a richer, more relaxed experience.

Advantages:

- Early morning and evening are much quieter, perfect for photography and enjoying the village atmosphere.

- More time to explore hiking trails, take boat rides, and visit the salt mine.

- Experience local hospitality in guesthouses and restaurants.

Accommodation Options:

- **Guesthouses:** Traditional and family-run, often with lake views.

- **Boutique Hotels:** Charming lodgings with modern amenities.

- **Vacation Rentals:** Cozy Alpine chalets and apartments.

Getting to Hallstatt

- **By Train:** Regular regional trains connect Salzburg to Hallstatt via Attnang-Puchheim and a short ferry ride.

- **By Car:** Scenic drives are beautiful but parking in Hallstatt is limited and often expensive.

- **By Bus:** Bus routes link Hallstatt with nearby towns.

Hallstatt offers an unforgettable blend of natural beauty, cultural heritage, and peaceful village life. Whether you admire it from the lakeside promenade, explore the depths of its ancient salt mines, hike surrounding Alpine trails, or capture its stunning views through your camera lens, this fairytale village will captivate your heart. Deciding between a day trip and an overnight stay depends on your travel style, but either choice promises a magical glimpse into Austria's authentic charm.

Chapter 6

The Austrian Alps – Adventures and Alpine Beauty

Austrian Alps

The Austrian Alps are synonymous with breathtaking mountain landscapes, outdoor adventures, and pristine nature. Stretching across the western and southern parts of the country, the Alps offer something for every season and every traveler—from adrenaline-pumping winter sports to peaceful summer hikes. This chapter will explore the best alpine regions for skiing and snowboarding, the summer

85

hiking trails and nature parks, the iconic Zell am See and Grossglockner High Alpine Road, luxurious spa resorts and wellness retreats, and essential safety tips for mountain travel.

Best Regions for Skiing and Snowboarding

Austria is world-renowned for its skiing and snowboarding, with perfectly groomed slopes, modern lifts, and vibrant mountain villages.

Top Ski Regions

- **St. Anton am Arlberg**: Often called the cradle of Alpine skiing, St. Anton is famous for its challenging slopes and lively après-ski scene. It is part of the Ski Arlberg area, Austria's largest interconnected ski region with over 300 km of pistes.

- **Kitzbühel**: Known for the legendary Hahnenkamm downhill race, Kitzbühel offers a combination of classic charm and modern facilities. Its slopes cater to all skill levels, making it popular with families and experts alike.

- **Sölden**: Located in the Ötztal Valley, Sölden boasts extensive glacier skiing and a buzzing nightlife. It regularly hosts World Cup ski races.

86

- **Zell am See-Kaprun:** This region combines lakeside beauty with ski resorts like Kitzsteinhorn Glacier, where snow is guaranteed most of the season.

Ski Season and Conditions

- The main ski season typically runs from December to April.

- Glacier resorts, like those in Sölden and Kaprun, often open earlier and close later due to permanent snow.

- Snowmaking equipment ensures good coverage, but always check real-time snow reports before planning.

Ski Schools and Equipment Rentals

- Most resorts offer ski schools for beginners and intermediate skiers.

- Equipment rental shops are widely available and usually provide the latest gear.

- Booking lessons or rentals in advance is recommended during peak times.

Summer Hiking Trails and Nature Parks

The Alps transform into a green paradise in summer, attracting hikers, mountain bikers, and nature lovers.

Popular Hiking Trails

- **Eagle Walk (Adlerweg):** A spectacular long-distance trail crossing Tyrol from west to east, covering about 413 kilometers with stunning panoramic views.

- **Alpe-Adria Trail:** This trail connects Austria with Italy and Slovenia, passing through diverse landscapes including alpine meadows and historic villages.

- **Krimml Waterfalls Trail:** A relatively easy hike leads to Europe's highest waterfalls, offering cool mist and stunning photographic opportunities.

- **Schwarzsee Lake Trail:** Near Zell am See, this circular trail offers tranquil lakeside views and wildflower meadows.

Nature Parks

- **Hohe Tauern National Park:** Austria's largest national park, home to the Grossglockner, the country's highest peak (3,798 meters). The park protects rare wildlife such as golden eagles, ibex, and marmots.

- **Gesäuse National Park:** Known for its rugged limestone peaks and the Enns River gorge, this park offers hiking, rafting, and rock climbing.

- **Dachstein Glacier Area:** Apart from skiing, it's an excellent summer destination for glacier hikes, cave tours, and via ferrata routes.

Tips for Summer Outdoor Activities

- Wear layered clothing and sturdy hiking boots.

- Carry water, sun protection, and a detailed map or GPS device.

- Be aware of weather changes—mountain weather can be unpredictable.

Zell am See and Grossglockner High Alpine Road

Zell am See

Nestled on the shores of Lake Zell, Zell am See is a charming alpine town that combines water sports, hiking, and skiing in one location.

89

- **Lake Zell:** In summer, the lake is perfect for swimming, sailing, and stand-up paddleboarding.

- **Schmittenhöhe Mountain:** Offers hundreds of kilometers of hiking trails and panoramic views.

- **Winter Activities:** Skiing on the nearby slopes, snowshoeing, and ice skating.

Grossglockner High Alpine Road

Grossglockner High Alpine Road view

One of the most scenic drives in Europe, the Grossglockner High Alpine Road takes you through spectacular mountain terrain and provides close views of Austria's highest peak.

90

- **Route Details:** The 48-kilometer toll road connects the states of Carinthia and Salzburg.

- **Viewpoints and Stops:** The route features numerous lookout points, visitor centers, and hiking trailheads.

- **Wildlife:** You might spot marmots, chamois, and golden eagles.

- **Visitor Tips:** The road is usually open from May to October, weather permitting.

Spa Resorts and Wellness Retreats

After days filled with mountain activities, the Austrian Alps offer many opportunities to relax and rejuvenate in world-class spa resorts and wellness retreats.

Popular Wellness Destinations

- **Bad Gastein:** Famous for its thermal springs and Belle Époque architecture, Bad Gastein has luxurious spa hotels and healing waters rich in radon.

- **Leogang:** Along with skiing and hiking, Leogang is home to wellness hotels offering saunas, massages, and holistic therapies.

91

- **Aqua Dome in Längenfeld:** A futuristic spa complex with thermal pools, outdoor infinity pools, and stunning mountain views.

Typical Wellness Treatments

- Thermal baths and mineral pools

- Traditional Austrian massages and aromatherapy

- Yoga and meditation sessions

- Alpine herbal treatments and mud wraps

Booking and Tips

- Spa resorts are popular year-round, so book well in advance, especially in winter and summer high seasons.

- Some resorts offer day passes for non-guests who want to enjoy spa facilities.

- Consider combining spa stays with active outdoor pursuits for a balanced vacation.

Safety Tips for Mountain Travel

Exploring the Austrian Alps is an unforgettable experience, but safety should always come first.

General Safety Advice

- **Weather Awareness:** Mountain weather changes rapidly. Check forecasts daily and be prepared for sudden rain, fog, or temperature drops.

- **Proper Gear:** Wear appropriate footwear, carry a map or GPS, extra layers, and enough food and water.

- **Inform Others:** Let someone know your plans if you hike or ski alone.

- **Altitude Acclimatization:** High altitudes may cause shortness of breath or dizziness. Take it slow and hydrate well.

Skiing and Snowboarding Safety

- Always wear a helmet and protective gear.

- Stay on marked trails suitable for your skill level.

- Follow resort safety rules and signs.

- Be mindful of other skiers and snowboarders.

Hiking and Wildlife

- Stick to designated trails.

93

- Don't approach wildlife; observe from a distance.

- Carry a whistle or other signaling device.

- Know emergency numbers (112 in Austria).

Driving on Mountain Roads

- Use low gears on steep roads.

- Watch for wildlife and cyclists.

- Check your vehicle's brakes and tires before trips.

- Be cautious in icy or snowy conditions.

The Austrian Alps are a spectacular destination that combines thrilling outdoor activities, stunning natural beauty, and restorative wellness experiences. Whether skiing on world-class slopes, hiking through emerald valleys, driving the iconic Grossglockner High Alpine Road, or unwinding in a thermal spa, the Alps provide year-round allure for all kinds of travelers. Prioritizing safety and proper planning will ensure your alpine adventure is as enjoyable as it is memorable.

Chapter 7

Graz and Styria – Culinary Delights and Green Hills

Nestled in the southeastern part of Austria, the region of Styria and its capital Graz offer a captivating blend of cultural richness, rolling green hills, and a culinary scene deeply rooted in tradition yet embracing modern flavors. Graz's UNESCO-listed Old Town combines medieval charm with contemporary vibrancy, while Styria is renowned for its vineyards, pumpkin seed oil, and local specialties. This chapter explores Graz's historic landmarks, the lush wine country, the famous Schlossberg hill, farmers' markets, regional cuisine, and the cultural events and festivals that bring the region to life.

UNESCO-listed Old Town

Graz's historic Old Town (Altstadt Graz) is one of Europe's best-preserved city centers and was declared a UNESCO World Heritage Site in 1999. Its streets reflect a harmonious blend of Gothic, Renaissance, and Baroque architecture, providing a picturesque backdrop for any visitor.

Key Highlights

95

- **Hauptplatz (Main Square):** The heart of Graz, this lively square is surrounded by historic buildings, cafés, and shops. It often hosts open-air markets and events.

- **Graz Cathedral (Dom):** A Gothic cathedral dating back to the 15th century, known for its richly decorated interior and unique blend of architectural styles.

- **Landhaus:** A Renaissance building housing the Styrian provincial parliament, famous for its beautiful arcaded courtyard.

- **Mausoleum of Emperor Ferdinand II:** An impressive example of early Baroque architecture, the mausoleum is notable for its ornate decorations and historical significance.

- **Murinsel (Island in the Mur):** A modern architectural marvel, this floating steel structure is an artificial island on the Mur River, featuring a café and amphitheater.

Walking Tours and Exploration

- Graz's compact Old Town is best explored on foot. Guided walking tours offer in-depth insight into the history, legends, and architectural evolution.

- Don't miss the chance to wander through narrow alleys like Sporgasse and Herrengasse, lined with

96

boutique shops and traditional cafés.

- At dusk, the illuminated buildings and lively street atmosphere create a magical experience.

Wine Country and Pumpkin Seed Oil

Styria, often called the "Green Heart of Austria," is famous for its fertile landscapes, vineyards, and unique regional products such as pumpkin seed oil.

Wine Regions

- The Styrian wine region is divided into three subregions: South Styria, West Styria, and East Styria, each offering distinct terroirs and wine styles.

- **South Styria** is especially popular for white wines such as Welschriesling, Sauvignon Blanc, and the region's signature, Muskateller.

- Wine estates offer tastings and cellar tours where visitors can sample exquisite varieties and learn about sustainable viticulture practices.

- The annual **Styrian Wine Road (Steirische Weinstraße)** is a scenic route winding through vineyards, picturesque villages, and rustic wine taverns (Buschenschank).

97

Pumpkin Seed Oil (Kürbiskernöl)

- This dark green, nutty-flavored oil is a regional specialty, made from roasted Styrian pumpkin seeds.

- Used as a salad dressing or finishing oil for soups and meats, it is prized both for its taste and health benefits.

- Visit local producers to see the traditional cold-pressing process and buy fresh oil to take home.

Schlossberg Hill and Clock Tower

Schlossberg Hill and Clock Tower view

One of Graz's most iconic landmarks, Schlossberg Hill offers panoramic views of the city and is a beloved green oasis.

98

The Clock Tower (Uhrturm)

- The 28-meter-tall clock tower dates back to the 13th century and is visible from many points around Graz.

- It features an unusual clock face where the large hand shows the hour, and the small hand shows minutes.

- The tower is accessible by foot via scenic trails or by funicular railway, which adds to the charm of the visit.

Activities on Schlossberg

- Enjoy leisurely walks through wooded paths and manicured gardens.

- Visit the **Schlossberg Caves** or enjoy a meal at one of the hilltop restaurants or cafés.

- Seasonal events, including open-air concerts and Christmas markets, are often held here.

Farmers' Markets and Regional Cuisine

99

Graz and Styria pride themselves on fresh, local produce and traditional recipes that reflect the region's agricultural heritage.

Farmers' Markets

- **Lendplatz Market:** A popular daily market in Graz offering fresh fruits, vegetables, cheese, meats, bread, and flowers.

- **Kaiser-Josef-Markt:** Another well-known market featuring local and organic products, artisanal baked goods, and street food stalls.

- Markets are great places to taste regional specialties and mingle with locals.

Regional Cuisine

- Styrian cuisine emphasizes fresh ingredients, simplicity, and hearty flavors.

- **Typical Dishes:**

  - **Backhendl:** Crispy fried chicken, often served with potato salad or cucumber salad.

  - **Steirisches Wurzelfleisch:** A traditional boiled pork dish with root vegetables.

  - **Käferbohnensalat:** A bean salad made with Käferbohnen (scarlet runner beans),

100

often dressed with pumpkin seed oil.

- **Riebel:** A cornmeal porridge typically served with milk, applesauce, or poppy seeds.

- Desserts include apple strudel and **Kaiserschmarrn**, a fluffy shredded pancake served with fruit compote.

Dining Tips

- Seek out Buschenschank taverns, seasonal wine taverns unique to the region, where homemade food and local wines are served in a cozy, rustic setting.

- Many restaurants in Graz combine traditional recipes with modern culinary creativity.

Cultural Events and Festivals

Graz and the wider Styrian region are culturally vibrant, with a calendar packed with festivals celebrating music, food, wine, and arts.

Key Festivals

- **Styrian Autumn Festival (Steirischer Herbst):** A major contemporary arts festival featuring theater,

101

visual arts, dance, and music from international and local artists.

- **La Strada Graz:** An annual street performance festival showcasing circus, theater, dance, and music.

- **Styriarte Festival:** A summer festival focused on classical and baroque music, often with performances held in historic venues.

- **Graz Wine Festival:** Celebrates the region's winemaking heritage with tastings, workshops, and food pairings.

- **Pumpkin Festival in Pöllauberg:** Held every October, this festival honors the pumpkin harvest with cooking demonstrations, contests, and family activities.

Local Traditions

- Traditional Styrian music includes folk songs accompanied by the harmonica, zither, and guitar.

- Dance and costume events keep the region's customs alive, often showcased during holiday celebrations.

Graz and Styria represent a perfect blend of historic charm, natural beauty, and culinary excellence. The UNESCO-listed Old Town offers a timeless journey

102

through history, while the surrounding green hills of Styria beckon with vineyards, pumpkin seed oil, and warm hospitality. Whether you're exploring the Schlossberg hill, savoring local delicacies at bustling farmers' markets, or immersing yourself in vibrant cultural festivals, this region invites you to experience Austria's heart in its most delicious and picturesque form.

103

Chapter 8

Innsbruck and Tyrol – Mountains, Sports, and Heritage

Innsbruck and Tyrol – Mountains views

Nestled in the heart of the Austrian Alps, Innsbruck and the surrounding Tyrol region are synonymous with majestic mountains, world-class winter sports, and a rich cultural heritage. Innsbruck, the capital of Tyrol, perfectly blends the charm of an alpine town with vibrant urban life. This chapter explores the city's iconic Old Town and its famous Golden Roof, the legacy of Olympic history and

104

winter sports, scenic hiking and biking routes, enduring local folk traditions, and excellent accommodation and dining options that make Tyrol a must-visit destination.

Innsbruck's Old Town and the Golden Roof

Innsbruck's Old Town (Altstadt) is a captivating blend of medieval and baroque architecture, surrounded by imposing mountain peaks. The city's most famous symbol, the **Golden Roof (Goldenes Dachl)**, stands proudly as a reminder of Innsbruck's imperial past.

The Golden Roof

- Constructed in the early 1500s for Emperor Maximilian I, the Golden Roof is adorned with 2,657 gilded copper tiles.

- It served as a royal box from which the Emperor and his wife could observe festivals, tournaments, and other public events.

- Today, the building houses a museum dedicated to Maximilian's reign, showcasing period artifacts, murals, and exhibits about Innsbruck's history.

- The intricate facade and the vibrant surrounding squares make it one of Austria's most photographed landmarks.

105

Exploring the Old Town

- **Maria-Theresien-Strasse:** The main pedestrian street, lined with elegant shops, cafés, and historic buildings.

- **St. Jacob's Cathedral (Dom zu St. Jakob):** A beautiful baroque cathedral featuring a richly decorated interior and frescoes by famous artists.

- **Hofkirche (Court Church):** Known for the impressive cenotaph of Emperor Maximilian I surrounded by 28 life-sized bronze statues of his ancestors and heroes.

- **City Tower (Stadtturm):** Climb 148 steps for panoramic views over Innsbruck's rooftops and the surrounding mountains.

- The Old Town buzzes with cultural events, street performers, and seasonal markets, especially during Christmas.

Olympic History and Winter Sports

Innsbruck's reputation as a winter sports capital is unparalleled. The city has twice hosted the Winter Olympics (1964 and 1976), making it a beacon for athletes and enthusiasts alike.

106

Olympic Legacy

- Innsbruck's Olympic venues have been maintained and upgraded, making the city a year-round hub for winter sports training and competition.

- The **Bergisel Ski Jump**, designed by architect Zaha Hadid, is an iconic landmark offering spectacular views and hosting international ski jumping events.

- The **Olympiaworld Innsbruck** complex includes ice rinks, swimming pools, and training facilities for various sports.

- The city's Olympic history is celebrated in museums and exhibitions, preserving memories of past games and inspiring future generations.

Winter Sports Opportunities

- Skiing and snowboarding are available in multiple nearby resorts, including the **Nordkette**, **Stubai Glacier**, and **Axamer Lizum**.

- Cross-country skiing trails wind through Tyrol's scenic valleys.

- Ice skating, tobogganing, and winter hiking trails add to the diverse activities available for visitors of all ages and skill levels.

107

Hiking and Biking Routes

Tyrol's mountainous terrain offers some of the best hiking and biking experiences in the Alps, catering to beginners, families, and seasoned adventurers.

Hiking

- The **Nordkette Nature Park** is just minutes from Innsbruck's city center and features trails with stunning alpine views.

- The **Eagle Walk (Adlerweg)** is a famous long-distance trail stretching over 400 kilometers across Tyrol, divided into manageable stages.

- Popular day hikes include the **Patscherkofel** mountain, the **Zirbenweg Trail** (a scenic pine trail), and the **Stubai High Trail**.

- Alpine huts (Almhütten) along the routes offer traditional Tyrolean hospitality with hearty food and warm drinks.

Biking

- Tyrol boasts extensive cycling networks, including flat valley routes and challenging mountain bike trails.

- The **Inn Valley Cycle Path** follows the Inn River and is ideal for family rides and casual cyclists.

- Mountain bikers can enjoy technical descents and cross-country trails around the **Serles Mountain** and **Kühtai**.

- Bike rentals and guided tours are widely available in Innsbruck and surrounding towns.

Local Folk Traditions

Tyrol's cultural identity is deeply rooted in its folk traditions, which thrive alongside modern life.

Traditional Clothing (Tracht)

- The Tyrolean **Tracht** is a colorful and intricate traditional costume, often worn during festivals and special events.

- Men typically wear lederhosen (leather shorts), embroidered shirts, and felt hats adorned with feathers.

- Women wear dirndls, dresses with bodices and aprons, often decorated with lace and floral motifs.

Music and Dance

109

- Alpine folk music, featuring instruments like the zither, accordion, and alphorn, is central to Tyrol's cultural life.

- Traditional dances such as the **Ländler** and **Schuhplattler** are performed during celebrations.

- Music festivals and folklore events throughout the year provide an immersive cultural experience.

Festivals and Customs

- **Almabtrieb:** The annual cattle drive in late September when decorated cows are brought down from mountain pastures to the valleys, celebrated with music, food, and parades.

- **Christmas Markets:** Innsbruck's Christmas markets are magical, with handcrafted gifts, mulled wine, and festive lights.

- **Tyrolean Festivals:** Events like the **Kundler Kirchtag** feature parades, traditional costumes, music, and local food specialties.

Accommodation and Dining Options

Visitors to Innsbruck and Tyrol are spoiled for choice with a variety of accommodation and dining experiences, from luxury hotels to charming alpine lodges, and from traditional inns to gourmet restaurants.

Accommodation

- **Luxury Hotels:** Innsbruck offers high-end hotels with mountain views, spa facilities, and easy access to ski lifts.

- **Alpine Lodges:** Traditional guesthouses and chalets provide a cozy atmosphere with rustic decor and home-cooked meals.

- **Budget Options:** Hostels and guesthouses in Innsbruck cater to backpackers and budget travelers.

- **Mountain Huts:** For hikers and bikers, alpine huts provide basic lodging and local hospitality in breathtaking settings.

Dining

- **Traditional Tyrolean Cuisine:** Restaurants serve specialties such as **Speck (smoked ham), Kaiserschmarrn (shredded pancake), Gröstl (fried potatoes with meat and onions)**, and hearty soups.

- **Fine Dining:** Innsbruck's gourmet restaurants combine local ingredients with international

111

culinary trends.

- **Cafés and Bakeries:** Enjoy freshly baked pastries, coffee, and the famous **Apfelstrudel** in cozy settings.

- **Local Breweries and Beer Gardens:** Sample Tyrol's craft beers and relax in scenic beer gardens during warmer months.

Innsbruck and Tyrol offer a compelling mix of alpine adventure, rich history, and vibrant culture. The city's Old Town with its Golden Roof and historic sites invites exploration, while the surrounding mountains provide endless opportunities for skiing, hiking, and biking. Tyrol's enduring folk traditions add color and warmth to the visitor experience, and its excellent accommodation and dining options ensure every traveler feels at home. Whether you come for the winter sports, the festivals, or simply to breathe in the fresh mountain air, Innsbruck and Tyrol will leave a lasting impression.

Chapter 9
Austrian Cuisine – A Tasting Journey

Austrian cuisine is a delicious reflection of the country's rich cultural history and diverse geography. From hearty mountain fare to elegant Viennese specialties, food in Austria is both comforting and sophisticated. This chapter takes you on a tasting journey through the must-try traditional dishes, iconic desserts, celebrated wines and beers, vegetarian and vegan options, and the best ways to immerse yourself in Austria's culinary heritage through food tours and cooking classes.

Must-Try Dishes

Austrian cuisine is famous for its generous portions, quality ingredients, and a balance of flavors rooted in Central European tradition. Here are some classic dishes you simply cannot miss:

Wiener Schnitzel

- **Description:** The iconic Wiener Schnitzel is a thin, breaded, and pan-fried veal cutlet, traditionally served with a lemon wedge and parsley potatoes or potato salad.

113

- **Origins:** This dish is synonymous with Vienna and considered Austria's national dish. Its roots trace back to the Italian cotoletta alla Milanese but the Wiener Schnitzel has evolved into a distinctly Austrian specialty.

- **Where to try:** Almost every traditional Austrian restaurant offers it, but the best versions are found in Viennese establishments such as Figlmüller and Plachutta.

- **Variations:** While veal is traditional, you'll also find pork or chicken schnitzels, often labeled as "Schnitzel Wiener Art."

Tafelspitz

- **Description:** Tafelspitz is boiled beef served in broth, often accompanied by horseradish, apple sauce, chive sauce, and roasted potatoes. The beef is typically a tender cut like rump or sirloin.

- **Cultural significance:** This dish was a favorite of Emperor Franz Joseph I and is considered a symbol of Viennese haute cuisine.

- **Where to try:** Traditional Viennese restaurants like Plachutta specialize in Tafelspitz, serving it with the authentic condiments and broth.

114

- **Serving style:** The beef is sliced thin and eaten with its rich consommé, making for a comforting, warming meal.

Kaiserschmarrn

- **Description:** Kaiserschmarrn is a light, fluffy shredded pancake sprinkled with powdered sugar and served with fruit compotes or plum sauce.

- **Name origin:** The name means "Emperor's Mess" and is said to have been a favorite dessert of Emperor Franz Joseph I.

- **How it's served:** It is often accompanied by stewed apple or berry sauces and sometimes nuts or raisins are added.

- **Where to try:** Available across Austria, especially in alpine huts, traditional inns, and dessert cafés.

Famous Desserts

Austrian desserts are renowned worldwide for their decadent flavors and beautiful presentation. Two of the most famous are Sachertorte and Apfelstrudel.

Sachertorte

115

- **Description:** Sachertorte is a dense chocolate cake with a layer of apricot jam, covered in a smooth, dark chocolate glaze.

- **Historical background:** Created in 1832 by Franz Sacher for Prince Metternich in Vienna, this cake has become a symbol of Viennese pastry craftsmanship.

- **Where to try:** The Hotel Sacher in Vienna is the most famous place to taste the original Sachertorte, but many cafés serve excellent versions.

- **Serving tip:** Traditionally enjoyed with a dollop of unsweetened whipped cream to balance the cake's richness.

Apfelstrudel

- **Description:** Apfelstrudel is a thin pastry filled with tart cooking apples, cinnamon, sugar, raisins, and breadcrumbs, baked to golden perfection.

- **Cultural roots:** This dessert has origins in the Austro-Hungarian Empire and is now a staple of Austrian cuisine.

- **Serving style:** Often served warm, sprinkled with powdered sugar, and accompanied by vanilla sauce, ice cream, or whipped cream.

- **Where to try:** Viennese cafés, alpine inns, and many restaurants throughout Austria serve Apfelstrudel, often made fresh daily.

Austrian Wines and Beers

Austria boasts a vibrant beverage culture, with wines and beers that complement its culinary offerings perfectly.

Austrian Wines

- **Regions:** The main wine-producing regions include **Wachau**, **Burgenland**, **Styria**, and the Vienna wine region (Wien).

- **Grape varieties:** Grüner Veltliner is the flagship white grape of Austria, known for its crisp acidity and peppery notes. Other varieties include Riesling, Zweigelt (red), and Blaufränkisch.

- **Wachau Valley:** Renowned for producing some of Austria's finest Grüner Veltliner and Rieslings, with terraced vineyards along the Danube River.

- **Wine tasting:** Many vineyards offer tours and tastings, especially in regions like Wachau and Burgenland. Small wine taverns called *Heurigen* in Vienna and the countryside invite visitors to enjoy local wines with simple food.

117

Austrian Beers

- **Beer styles:** Austria produces a variety of lagers, pilsners, and wheat beers. Popular styles include Märzen and Vienna Lager.

- **Famous breweries:** Some well-known Austrian breweries include Stiegl, Ottakringer, Gösser, and Egger.

- **Local specialties:** Regional beers vary in flavor; alpine breweries often craft beers with pure mountain spring water, giving them unique freshness.

- **Beer culture:** Inns and beer gardens throughout Austria offer lively atmospheres to sample beers, often accompanied by traditional snacks like pretzels or cheese.

Vegetarian and Vegan Options

While Austrian cuisine is traditionally meat-heavy, the growing demand for vegetarian and vegan dishes has led to exciting culinary developments.

Vegetarian Dishes

- **Käsespätzle:** A hearty dish of soft egg noodles layered with melted cheese and topped with crispy

118

onions, similar to mac and cheese.

- **Knödel (dumplings):** Potato or bread dumplings served with mushroom sauces or in vegetable soups.

- **Vegetarian soups:** Seasonal vegetable soups made from fresh local produce.

- **Salads and sides:** Austrian meals often include fresh salads and vegetable sides such as sauerkraut or red cabbage.

Vegan Options

- **Growing availability:** Especially in urban centers like Vienna, Graz, and Salzburg, vegan restaurants and cafés are increasingly popular.

- **Vegan adaptations:** Many traditional dishes have vegan versions, such as schnitzels made from seitan or tofu and vegan pastries.

- **Farmers markets:** Local markets offer fresh fruits, vegetables, nuts, and grains, providing excellent ingredients for vegan cooking.

- **Culinary events:** Festivals and pop-up food markets often feature vegan options highlighting Austrian ingredients and international influences.

Food Tours and Cooking Classes

To fully experience Austrian cuisine, participating in food tours and cooking classes offers an immersive and memorable experience.

Food Tours

- **Vienna Food Tours:** Explore the city's culinary landscape by visiting traditional markets like the **Naschmarkt**, tasting street food, café pastries, and local specialties.

- **Salzburg and Innsbruck Tours:** These tours combine sightseeing with visits to artisan food producers, cheese makers, and breweries.

- **Alpine Food Tours:** In regions like Tyrol and Salzburg, tours often include tastings of mountain cheeses, cured meats, and schnapps.

Cooking Classes

- **Learn to cook classic dishes:** Many culinary schools and restaurants offer half-day or full-day classes teaching how to prepare Wiener Schnitzel, Apfelstrudel, and other Austrian classics.

- **Hands-on experience:** Classes typically include a market visit to select fresh ingredients, followed by guided cooking and tasting sessions.

- **Specialized classes:** Some focus on baking Viennese pastries or exploring vegan Austrian cuisine.

- **Private and group options:** Whether you prefer an intimate session or a social group experience, options are available across Austria's major cities.

Austrian cuisine invites you to savor a rich and diverse culinary tradition steeped in history and regional flavors. From the crispy, golden Wiener Schnitzel to the sweet decadence of Sachertorte, each dish tells a story of Austria's cultural heritage. Pair these with excellent wines from the Wachau or refreshing beers from alpine breweries, and you have a truly authentic gastronomic experience.

For those with dietary preferences, Austria is increasingly accommodating vegetarian and vegan lifestyles without compromising on flavor. Finally, engaging in food tours and cooking classes provides a unique, hands-on way to connect with Austrian culture and bring a taste of Austria back home with you.

121

Chapter 10
Festivals and Traditions

Austria is a land steeped in rich cultural heritage, where festivals and traditions play a vital role in the social and cultural fabric of the nation. Throughout the year, Austrians celebrate their history, religion, and seasonal changes with events that attract both locals and visitors alike. From the glamorous Vienna Opera Ball to the cozy and magical Christmas markets, Austria's festivals offer a unique glimpse into its customs and communal spirit. This chapter explores some of the most iconic festivals and traditions, seasonal celebrations, and essential etiquette tips to help you navigate Austria's cultural events respectfully and enjoyably.

Vienna Opera Ball and Salzburg Festival

Vienna Opera Ball

- **Overview:** The Vienna Opera Ball (*Wiener Opernball*) is one of the most prestigious and elegant social events in Austria, held annually at the Vienna State Opera in February or March. It epitomizes the grandeur of Viennese culture and aristocratic tradition.

- **History:** The ball dates back to the 19th century and has evolved into a major event attracting international celebrities, dignitaries, and guests from around the world.

- **What to expect:** Guests dress in formal evening wear—tuxedos for men and long gowns for women—and the event features classical music performances, traditional waltzing, and a grand procession.

- **Experience:** The ball opens with the debutantes' dance, followed by a night of music, dance, and socializing. The atmosphere is sophisticated, embodying Vienna's classical music and aristocratic roots.

- **Tips for visitors:** Tickets are highly sought after and should be booked well in advance. Even if you don't attend, the area around the opera house buzzes with pre- and post-ball excitement, and special viewing events sometimes take place nearby.

Salzburg Festival

- **Overview:** The Salzburg Festival (*Salzburger Festspiele*) is one of the world's most renowned music and drama festivals, held every summer in Salzburg, the birthplace of Mozart.

123

- **History:** Founded in 1920, it celebrates classical music, opera, and theater with performances by world-class artists.

- **Highlights:** The festival features opera productions, orchestral concerts, and theatrical plays, often held in historic venues like the Felsenreitschule and the Großes Festspielhaus.

- **Mozart Connection:** Salzburg's deep connection to Mozart is celebrated through performances of his operas and compositions, making the festival a pilgrimage for classical music lovers.

- **Visiting tips:** The festival attracts thousands of visitors, so booking tickets early is essential. Besides the performances, the city's atmosphere is vibrant with outdoor concerts, exhibitions, and cultural events.

Christmas Markets and Winter Traditions

Christmas Markets (*Christkindlmärkte*)

- **Overview:** Austria's Christmas markets are among the most enchanting in Europe, transforming towns and cities into winter wonderlands from late November until Christmas.

124

- **Famous markets:** Vienna's Christkindlmarkt at Rathausplatz, Salzburg's Christkindlmarkt, and Innsbruck's Old Town Market are some of the most popular.

- **Atmosphere:** Stalls sell handcrafted gifts, ornaments, festive foods like roasted chestnuts and gingerbread, and warm drinks such as Glühwein (mulled wine).

- **Family activities:** Many markets offer ice skating, nativity scenes, and traditional music, making them ideal for families.

- **Regional variations:** Each region has unique crafts and specialties; for example, Styria is known for its Christmas straw decorations.

Winter Traditions

- **Advent customs:** The four weeks leading up to Christmas are marked by the lighting of Advent candles and the preparation of Advent calendars.

- **Krampus Runs:** In early December, some Alpine regions host *Krampus* parades where people dress as the mythical creature Krampus, who punishes naughty children. This tradition blends folklore with festive celebration.

- **New Year's Eve:** Austrians celebrate *Silvester* with fireworks, concerts, and parties, especially in

125

Vienna where the *New Year's Eve Trail* offers live music and street festivities.

Easter in Austria

- **Religious significance:** Easter is one of the most important religious holidays in Austria, marked by church services, family gatherings, and traditional customs.

- **Easter markets:** Similar to Christmas markets, Easter markets sell painted eggs, handmade decorations, and seasonal foods.

- **Egg traditions:** Decorating Easter eggs (*Ostereier*) is a cherished activity. Eggs are often hand-painted with intricate designs, including symbolic motifs like flowers and animals.

- **Easter fires and processions:** In some regions, Easter fires (*Osterfeuer*) are lit to symbolize the resurrection of Christ and the coming of spring.

- **Special foods:** Typical Easter dishes include lamb, ham, and sweet bread called *Osterpinze*.

Harvest Celebrations and Regional Festivities

Harvest Festivals (*Erntedankfest*)

- **Overview:** Celebrated in autumn, these festivals thank the harvest gods for a bountiful crop and feature church services, parades, and traditional music.

- **Customs:** Decorations made of grains, fruits, and vegetables are common, symbolizing abundance and gratitude.

- **Community events:** Many villages hold fairs, complete with traditional costumes, folk dances, and local food and drink.

Regional Traditions

- **Carnival (*Fasching*):** The pre-Lenten carnival season is celebrated with masquerade balls, street parades, and humorous performances, especially vibrant in regions like Carinthia and Vienna.

- **Alpine customs:** Mountain regions such as Tyrol and Vorarlberg maintain unique folk traditions including yodeling, traditional costumes (*Tracht*), and alphorn playing.

- **May Day**: May 1st is celebrated with dancing around maypoles, singing, and outdoor festivities welcoming spring.

Cultural Etiquette at Events

Understanding local customs and etiquette will help you enjoy Austria's festivals and traditions fully and respectfully.

Dress Code

- **Formal events:** For events like the Vienna Opera Ball, formal evening wear is mandatory. Long dresses for women and tuxedos or dark suits for men are standard.

- **Traditional attire:** At many festivals, especially in rural or Alpine areas, locals wear traditional Austrian clothing such as dirndls and lederhosen. Visitors are welcome to wear these but should do so respectfully.

- **Casual festivals:** For outdoor markets and fairs, smart casual dress with comfortable shoes is advisable due to walking and weather.

Behavior and Participation

128

- **Respect religious observances:** Many festivals have religious origins; showing respect during ceremonies or church services is important.

- **Joining in:** Austrians appreciate visitors who engage with traditions, whether it's dancing at a festival or trying local foods, but it's polite to observe before participating.

- **Photography:** Always ask permission before photographing people, especially during religious or intimate ceremonies.

- **Punctuality:** Austrians value punctuality, especially for formal events and performances.

Social Interactions

- **Greetings:** A polite handshake and eye contact are customary when meeting people at events.

- **Language:** While German is the official language, English is widely understood in tourist areas. Learning a few basic German phrases related to greetings and thanks is appreciated.

- **Tipping:** It is customary to tip around 5-10% in restaurants and to those providing services during events or markets.

129

Austria's festivals and traditions offer a captivating insight into the country's history, culture, and communal spirit. Whether you attend the opulent Vienna Opera Ball, immerse yourself in the joyous Salzburg Festival, wander through the magical Christmas markets, or witness the vibrant harvest celebrations, each event is an opportunity to experience Austria's unique blend of old-world charm and modern vitality.

By understanding the customs, respecting local etiquette, and participating wholeheartedly, you will enrich your travel experience and connect deeply with Austrian culture. Festivals here are not just events; they are living traditions that bring communities together and create unforgettable memories for visitors.

130

Chapter 11
Art, Architecture, and Museums

Austria's rich cultural heritage is vividly expressed through its art, architecture, and museums. From the grand imperial palaces of Vienna to cutting-edge contemporary galleries, Austria offers an extraordinary journey through artistic achievements spanning centuries. The country's cities are living museums, showcasing styles from Gothic and Baroque to modernist and avant-garde, reflecting Austria's historical significance as a cultural crossroads in Europe. This chapter explores Austria's iconic architectural landmarks, world-class museums, and the artistic treasures they hold, guiding you to the best cultural experiences during your visit.

Imperial Architecture: Baroque and Gothic Marvels

Austria's architectural landscape is dominated by imperial grandeur and historic styles that tell the story of its past rulers and cultural evolution.

Baroque Splendor

- **Origins:** The Baroque style flourished in Austria during the 17th and 18th centuries, especially

131

under the Habsburg dynasty, which sought to express power and religious devotion through elaborate architecture.

- **Characteristics:** Baroque buildings feature grand staircases, ornate facades, intricate stucco work, and richly decorated interiors with frescoes and gilded details.

- **Key examples:**

  - **Schönbrunn Palace (Vienna):** Former imperial summer residence with sprawling gardens, opulent rooms, and the world's oldest zoo.

  - **Melk Abbey (Lower Austria):** A Benedictine abbey perched on a hill overlooking the Danube, famous for its impressive library and frescoed ceilings.

  - **St. Peter's Church (Vienna):** A masterpiece of Baroque church architecture with a dramatic dome and lavish interior.

Gothic Heritage

- **Period:** Austria's Gothic architecture dates back to the Middle Ages, often associated with religious and civic buildings.

132

- **Features:** Pointed arches, ribbed vaults, flying buttresses, and stained-glass windows are hallmarks of Gothic style.

- **Prominent sites:**

  - **St. Stephen's Cathedral (Vienna):** The city's iconic symbol, featuring a multi-colored tiled roof and soaring Gothic spires. Climbing the tower offers panoramic views of Vienna.

  - **Graz Cathedral:** Known for its late Gothic interior and impressive altarpieces.

  - **Burg Kreuzenstein (Lower Austria):** A reconstructed medieval castle showcasing Gothic elements combined with romanticized architecture.

The Belvedere and Kunsthistorisches Museum

Austria's museums house some of the world's finest collections of art, offering deep insights into European history and creativity.

The Belvedere Palace

133

- **Overview:** The Belvedere is a historic complex of two Baroque palaces in Vienna—the Upper and Lower Belvedere—set within expansive gardens.

- **Collections:** The Upper Belvedere hosts an impressive collection of Austrian art, from medieval times to contemporary works.

- **Highlights:**

  o **Gustav Klimt:** The museum's star attraction is Klimt's masterpiece *The Kiss*, a symbol of Viennese Secession art.

  o **Egon Schiele and Oskar Kokoschka:** Works by these expressionist painters offer a raw and emotional glimpse into early 20th-century Austria.

- **Gardens:** The French-style gardens between the palaces provide a serene environment for visitors, featuring fountains, sculptures, and meticulously manicured paths.

Kunsthistorisches Museum (Museum of Art History)

- **Significance:** One of the world's leading art museums, the Kunsthistorisches Museum in Vienna was founded by Emperor Franz Joseph I to

134

display the Habsburgs' extensive collections.

- **Collections:** The museum spans centuries and styles, featuring Egyptian and Near Eastern art, classical antiquities, Renaissance and Baroque masterpieces.

- **Masterpieces:**

    - **Peter Paul Rubens:** The museum holds one of the largest collections of Rubens' works.

    - **Titian and Vermeer:** Renaissance and Dutch Golden Age paintings.

    - **Old Masters:** Paintings by Raphael, Caravaggio, and Velázquez.

- **Architecture:** The building itself is a masterpiece of Renaissance Revival architecture, with an ornate interior adorned with grand staircases and frescoes.

Modern Art and Contemporary Spaces

Austria's art scene is not confined to historic works; it is vibrant and evolving with contemporary and modern art showcased in innovative spaces.

135

MuseumsQuartier Vienna

- **Overview:** One of the largest cultural complexes in the world, MuseumsQuartier (MQ) in Vienna combines baroque buildings with modern architecture.

- **Highlights:**

  - **Leopold Museum:** Home to the world's largest Egon Schiele collection and works by Gustav Klimt.

  - **MUMOK:** Museum of Modern Art Ludwig Foundation Vienna, focusing on contemporary art from the 20th and 21st centuries.

  - **Contemporary cultural programs:** MQ hosts exhibitions, festivals, film screenings, and performances, creating a dynamic cultural hub.

MAK – Austrian Museum of Applied Arts / Contemporary Art

- **Focus:** MAK bridges traditional applied arts and contemporary design.

136

- **Collections:** Furniture, textiles, ceramics, and graphic arts from the 19th century to today.

- **Design:** The museum features exhibitions on architecture, fashion, and multimedia art.

Kunsthalle Wien

- **Role:** An important venue for contemporary art, focusing on innovative, experimental exhibitions.

- **Programs:** Rotating exhibitions by Austrian and international artists, educational programs, and community engagement.

Historic Libraries and Palaces

Austria's libraries and palatial estates offer a glimpse into the intellectual and aristocratic life of past centuries.

Austrian National Library

- **Location:** Housed in the Hofburg Palace in Vienna.

- **Significance:** One of the world's most beautiful historic libraries, with a magnificent Baroque State Hall featuring ceiling frescoes, marble statues, and thousands of ancient volumes.

- **Collections:** Manuscripts, maps, globes, and rare books spanning centuries of European history and scholarship.

Hofburg Palace

- **Overview:** The former imperial palace in the heart of Vienna, Hofburg served as the winter residence of the Habsburg dynasty.

- **Attractions:** Imperial Apartments, the Sisi Museum dedicated to Empress Elisabeth, and the Spanish Riding School.

- **Architecture:** The palace combines Gothic, Renaissance, Baroque, and Rococo styles, reflecting its centuries-long development.

Schloss Eggenberg (Graz)

- **Highlights:** A UNESCO World Heritage site, this palace features exquisite Baroque architecture and richly decorated interiors.

- **The Planetary Room:** Symbolizes the harmony of the cosmos through its ceiling paintings and design.

UNESCO World Heritage Sites

138

Austria is home to numerous UNESCO World Heritage sites that preserve its cultural and natural treasures.

Historic Centre of Vienna

- **Description:** Vienna's historic center is a blend of Roman, medieval, and Baroque architecture.

- **Highlights:** St. Stephen's Cathedral, the Hofburg, the Ringstrasse boulevard with its palaces, theaters, and museums.

- **Cultural significance:** Vienna's center reflects its role as the capital of the Austro-Hungarian Empire and its ongoing influence in European art and politics.

Hallstatt-Dachstein / Salzkammergut Cultural Landscape

- **Features:** Famous for the picturesque village of Hallstatt, salt mines, and dramatic Alpine landscapes.

- **Significance:** This site illustrates human settlement and salt mining dating back thousands of years.

Wachau Cultural Landscape

- **Location:** Along the Danube River between Melk and Krems.

139

- **Highlights:** Vineyards, medieval towns, castles, and monasteries.

- **Relevance:** Showcases the interaction of natural beauty with human culture, particularly viticulture.

Schönbrunn Palace and Gardens

- **Recognition:** Included in the UNESCO list for its architectural and historical importance.

- **Attractions:** Extensive gardens, the Gloriette, and the world's oldest zoo.

Tips for Visiting Museums and Architectural Sites

- **Plan ahead:** Many popular museums and palaces require advance ticket bookings, especially in peak tourist seasons.

- **Guided tours:** Consider joining guided tours for deeper historical and artistic context.

- **Opening hours:** Museums often close one day a week (usually Monday), so check before planning your visit.

- **Photography:** Some museums restrict photography, especially flash or tripods. Always check signage.

- **Accessibility:** Many museums and sites offer facilities for visitors with disabilities, but some historic buildings may have limited access.

Austria's artistic and architectural heritage is a cornerstone of its cultural identity, offering visitors a vast spectrum of experiences from the opulent imperial past to vibrant contemporary creativity. Whether you marvel at the intricate Baroque details of Schönbrunn Palace, stand beneath the soaring Gothic spires of St. Stephen's Cathedral, or immerse yourself in modern art at MuseumsQuartier, you are witnessing layers of history and innovation.

Chapter 12
Austria's Natural Wonders

Austria is not only a land of imperial palaces and cultural treasures but also a country blessed with stunning natural beauty. From thundering waterfalls and mysterious ice caves to serene lakes and vast national parks, Austria's landscapes offer countless opportunities for outdoor exploration and relaxation. The country's commitment to sustainability ensures that these natural wonders are preserved for future generations while providing visitors with a chance to connect with nature in a responsible way.

This chapter highlights some of Austria's most spectacular natural sites, explores the diverse ecosystems protected in its national parks, and offers tips on how to enjoy outdoor activities such as cycling and hiking while respecting the environment.

Krimml Waterfalls and Eisriesenwelt Ice Caves

Krimml Waterfalls

Krimml Waterfalls view

- **Overview:** Located in the Hohe Tauern National Park, the Krimml Waterfalls are Europe's highest waterfalls, cascading down in three stages over a total height of 380 meters (1,247 feet).

- **Experience:** Visitors can follow well-maintained hiking trails alongside the falls, taking in the powerful rush of water and the mist that cools the air. The trails offer several viewpoints, each providing unique perspectives on the falls and the surrounding lush Alpine forest.

- **Best Time to Visit:** Late spring to early autumn, when the water flow is strongest due to melting snow. Winter visits offer a more tranquil but icy landscape.

- **Nearby Attractions:** The Krimml village offers charming accommodations, local restaurants, and access to other hiking routes in the National Park.

143

Eisriesenwelt Ice Caves

Eisriesenwelt Ice Caves view

- **Introduction:** Near Werfen, about 40 kilometers south of Salzburg, the Eisriesenwelt ("World of the Ice Giants") is the largest ice cave system in the world, extending over 42 kilometers into the mountain.

- **Tour Highlights:** Visitors take a cable car and then hike up to the cave entrance before entering the icy chambers where spectacular ice formations—stalactites, stalagmites, and frozen waterfalls—create an otherworldly atmosphere.

- **Temperature:** The cave remains below freezing year-round, so warm clothing is essential.

144

- **Access and Safety:** Guided tours last about 75 minutes and include explanations of the cave's geology and history. Due to the fragile nature of the formations, visitors are asked to follow strict guidelines to protect the environment.

Lakes Worth Visiting: Wolfgangsee, Neusiedler See

Austria's lakes are among its most beloved natural attractions, each with its own character, activities, and scenic charm.

Wolfgangsee

Wolfgangsee lake view

145

- **Location:** Situated in the Salzkammergut region, Wolfgangsee is known for its crystal-clear water, mountain backdrop, and traditional lakeside villages such as St. Wolfgang and St. Gilgen.

- **Activities:** Swimming, sailing, paddleboarding, and hiking around the lake's perimeter. The Schafberg Mountain offers a cog railway and panoramic views over the lake and surrounding Alps.

- **Cultural Highlights:** The lakeside towns feature baroque churches, local crafts, and open-air festivals in summer.

- **Accommodation:** From lakeside resorts to cozy guesthouses, Wolfgangsee caters to a range of visitors.

Neusiedler See

Neusiedler See view

146

- **Overview:** Located on the border with Hungary in the Burgenland region, Neusiedler See is Central Europe's largest steppe lake and a UNESCO World Heritage site.

- **Ecology:** The shallow lake and surrounding wetlands provide critical habitat for over 300 species of birds and diverse flora.

- **Recreation:** Popular for windsurfing, sailing, and cycling around the lake's flat terrain.

- **Wine Region:** The area around Neusiedler See is known for its vineyards and wine festivals, adding a cultural dimension to the natural experience.

National Parks and Biodiversity

Austria is home to several national parks that protect its rich biodiversity and offer visitors immersive nature experiences.

Hohe Tauern National Park

- **Size and Scope:** The largest national park in Austria, spanning over 1,800 square kilometers across Carinthia, Salzburg, and Tyrol.

- **Landscape:** Alpine peaks, glaciers, rivers, and valleys.

- **Wildlife:** Home to golden eagles, ibex, chamois, marmots, and lynx. Efforts have been successful in reintroducing the bearded vulture.

- **Visitor Centers:** Provide educational exhibits, guided tours, and information about conservation.

- **Activities:** Hiking, wildlife watching, mountain biking, and educational nature walks.

Gesäuse National Park

Gesäuse National Park view

148

- **Location:** In Styria, characterized by rugged limestone peaks and deep gorges.

- **Highlights:** Offers challenging hiking and climbing routes with breathtaking views.

- **Flora and Fauna:** Includes rare orchids, chamois, and the elusive black stork.

Thayatal National Park

Thayatal National Park view

- **Location:** On the border with the Czech Republic, this park preserves a unique forest landscape along the Thaya River.

- **Biodiversity:** Known for its rich plant life and bird species.

- **Activities:** Walking trails, birdwatching, and river kayaking.

149

Cycling and Nature Trails

Austria's well-developed network of cycling and hiking trails makes it easy to explore its diverse landscapes at your own pace.

Cycling Trails

- **Danube Cycle Path (Donauradweg):** One of Europe's most famous bike routes, stretching along the Danube River from Passau (Germany) to Vienna and beyond. It passes through vineyards, historic towns, and nature reserves.

- **Salzkammergut Cycle Path:** Offers a scenic ride around lakes, past castles, and through Alpine foothills.

- **Lake Neusiedl Circuit:** Flat and family-friendly, ideal for all ages and skill levels.

Hiking and Walking Trails

- **Eagle Walk:** A long-distance trail through the Tyrolean Alps featuring varied terrain and stunning views.

- **Alpe Adria Trail:** Connecting the Alps to the Adriatic Sea, passing through Austria, Slovenia, and Italy.

150

- **Local Nature Trails:** Many regions have shorter, well-marked trails suitable for casual walks or day hikes, often with information boards explaining local flora, fauna, and history.

Sustainable Travel in Austria

Austria is committed to sustainable tourism, balancing visitor enjoyment with environmental preservation and local community support.

Eco-Friendly Practices

- **Green Transportation:** Extensive public transport networks including trains, trams, and buses reduce the need for car travel. Many cities offer bike-sharing schemes.

- **Eco-Certified Accommodations:** Austria has numerous hotels and guesthouses with eco-certifications, emphasizing energy efficiency, waste reduction, and local sourcing.

- **Nature Protection:** Visitors are encouraged to respect wildlife, stay on marked trails, and avoid littering. Many parks have rules to minimize human impact.

Responsible Tourism Tips

151

- **Support Local:** Choose local guides, crafts, and food to contribute to the economy and cultural preservation.

- **Pack Light and Smart:** Reduce waste by using reusable water bottles and minimizing plastic.

- **Seasonal Travel:** Visiting during shoulder seasons helps avoid overcrowding and supports year-round local businesses.

- **Respect Traditions:** Learn about regional customs and follow guidelines in natural and cultural sites.

Austria's natural wonders—from its majestic waterfalls and ice caves to its pristine lakes and expansive national parks—offer unforgettable experiences for nature lovers and adventure seekers. The country's dedication to sustainability means that visitors can explore these treasures while helping to protect them.

Whether cycling along the Danube, hiking through the Hohe Tauern, or simply relaxing by Wolfgangsee, Austria invites you to immerse yourself in its breathtaking landscapes and vibrant ecosystems. Embrace the chance to connect with nature responsibly and discover the diverse beauty that makes Austria an exceptional destination for outdoor enthusiasts.

Chapter 13
Getting Around Austria

Austria boasts an excellent transportation system that allows travelers to explore its vibrant cities, quaint villages, and breathtaking landscapes with ease and comfort. Whether you prefer the convenience of trains and public transit, the freedom of driving yourself, or using regional transport passes, Austria's infrastructure is well developed and tourist-friendly. This chapter will guide you through the best ways to get around the country, offering practical tips on trains, driving, car rentals, scenic routes, regional passes, accessibility, and useful transportation apps.

Trains and Public Transit

Austria's Rail Network

Austria's rail system is renowned for its punctuality, comfort, and extensive coverage. The **Österreichische Bundesbahnen (ÖBB)** is the national railway operator, connecting major cities and smaller towns efficiently. Trains range from high-speed rail to regional services, making it easy to tailor your journey depending on your schedule and budget.

- **High-Speed Rail:** The Railjet trains connect Vienna, Salzburg, Innsbruck, Graz, and other key cities at speeds up to 230 km/h (143 mph). These

153

trains offer first and second-class seating, onboard dining, free Wi-Fi, and power outlets.

- **Regional Trains:** Regionalexpress (REX) and Regionalbahn (R) services link smaller towns and scenic routes, perfect for exploring Austria's countryside.

- **Night Trains:** Nightjet services provide overnight connections to and from Austria to other European countries like Germany, Italy, and Switzerland.

Major Train Routes

- **Vienna to Salzburg:** One of the most popular routes, the Railjet train takes about 2.5 hours, offering views of the Danube Valley and Alpine foothills.

- **Salzburg to Innsbruck:** A scenic journey through the Tyrolean Alps, this route is ideal for travelers heading to ski resorts or mountain adventures.

- **Vienna to Graz:** This route crosses the southeastern region and connects the cultural hubs of Austria.

Urban Public Transit

Austria's cities feature comprehensive public transit networks including subways (U-Bahn), trams, and buses.

154

- **Vienna:** The Vienna U-Bahn has five lines covering the city, complemented by an extensive tram and bus system. Tickets are valid across modes and can be purchased at machines or via apps.

- **Salzburg:** Trams and buses serve the city and nearby suburbs, making it easy to reach major attractions such as the Fortress Hohensalzburg and Mozart's birthplace.

- **Graz:** Offers trams and buses that provide convenient access to the city center, Schlossberg, and museums.

Tickets and Fare Systems

- **Single Tickets:** Valid for one journey on any mode of public transport.

- **Day Passes:** Unlimited travel within a city for 24 hours.

- **Weekly and Monthly Passes:** Cost-effective options for longer stays.

- **ÖBB Tickets:** Can be purchased online, at stations, or via the ÖBB app. Early booking often provides discounted fares.

155

Driving and Road Tips

Driving in Austria

Renting a car can be an excellent choice if you want to explore rural areas, mountain passes, or follow scenic routes at your own pace. However, it's important to understand Austria's driving regulations and road conditions before hitting the road.

- **Driving Side:** Austria drives on the right side of the road.

- **Speed Limits:** Generally, 50 km/h (31 mph) in cities, 100 km/h (62 mph) on rural roads, and 130 km/h (81 mph) on highways (Autobahns). Always observe posted signs.

- **Road Signs:** Use standard European road signs. Familiarize yourself with key signs, including priority rules at intersections and warnings for wildlife or sharp bends.

- **Tolls and Vignettes:** Austria requires a motorway vignette (toll sticker) for driving on highways. These can be purchased at border crossings, gas stations, or online. Additional tolls apply for some tunnels and alpine passes.

- **Winter Driving:** From November to April, winter tires or chains are mandatory in snowy or icy

156

conditions. Mountain roads may require extra
caution.

Parking

- **City Parking:** Look for blue zones where parking
  is limited to a few hours with a parking disc, or
  paid parking garages and lots.

- **Park and Ride:** Many cities offer park-and-ride
  facilities near public transit hubs, allowing you to
  park outside the city center and use public
  transport to avoid congestion.

Car Rentals and Scenic Routes

Renting a Car

- **Requirements:** Drivers must be at least 18 years
  old (age may vary by rental company), hold a valid
  driver's license, and often a credit card for the
  deposit.

- **Rental Companies:** International agencies like
  Hertz, Europcar, Sixt, and Avis operate throughout
  Austria, including at airports and train stations.

- **Insurance:** Basic insurance is included, but
  consider additional coverage for peace of mind.

157

- **Manual vs. Automatic**: Manual transmission cars are more common and generally cheaper, but automatics are widely available.

- **Fuel Policy**: Understand the fuel policy (full-to-full is common) to avoid extra charges.

Scenic Driving Routes

Austria is famous for its stunning drives that offer breathtaking views of mountains, lakes, and quaint villages.

- **Grossglockner High Alpine Road**: This panoramic toll road climbs to over 2,500 meters, winding past glaciers, waterfalls, and alpine meadows. Stops along the way include visitor centers and hiking trails.

- **Romantic Road (Romantikstraße)**: This route meanders through picturesque towns like Hallstatt and Salzburg, perfect for lovers of history and nature.

- **Salzkammergut Lake District**: Drive around Wolfgangsee, Hallstätter See, and Traunsee for idyllic lake views, castles, and hiking opportunities.

- **Nockalm Road**: A scenic mountain road through the Nockberge Biosphere Reserve, featuring gentle

158

alpine landscapes and rich biodiversity.

- **Weinstrasse (Wine Road):** Located in the Burgenland region, this route passes vineyards, wine taverns, and charming villages.

Regional Transport Passes

Why Use a Transport Pass?

Austria offers a variety of regional and national transport passes that provide convenience, flexibility, and savings for travelers planning to explore extensively by public transport.

Key Passes

- **ÖBB Vorteilscard:** A discount card offering up to 50% off train fares for a year. Ideal for frequent train travelers.

- **Austrian Rail Pass:** Provides a set number of train travel days within a given period, allowing unlimited train travel on those days.

- **Vienna Card:** Unlimited travel on Vienna's public transport plus discounts on museums, attractions, and restaurants.

- **Salzburg Card:** Includes public transport, free admission to many museums, and discounts on local activities.

- **Salzkammergut Card:** For travelers exploring the lake district, it offers free or discounted entry to attractions and access to local transport.

- **Burgenland Card:** Covers public transportation and entry to castles, museums, and wine tastings in Burgenland.

How to Buy and Use Passes

Most passes are available online, at train stations, tourist offices, or via mobile apps. They can be paper tickets or digital, and sometimes require activation on the first use.

Accessibility and Transportation Apps

Accessibility

Austria strives to make transportation accessible to all, including travelers with reduced mobility.

- **Train Stations:** Many major stations have elevators, ramps, and tactile guidance paths for the visually impaired.

- **Public Transport:** Low-floor trams and buses are common in cities like Vienna and Salzburg, with designated spaces for wheelchairs.

- **Assistance Services:** ÖBB offers assistance for boarding and disembarking trains if arranged in advance (at least 24 hours notice).

- **Accessible Facilities:** Most airports, train stations, and major bus terminals provide accessible toilets and parking spaces.

Useful Transportation Apps

Technology greatly enhances the ease of travel in Austria. Here are some key apps to download before or during your trip:

- **ÖBB App:** The official app for Austria's railways; allows booking tickets, viewing schedules, real-time train updates, and platform changes.

- **WienMobil:** Vienna's public transport app providing route planning, ticket purchases, and real-time updates for U-Bahn, tram, and buses.

- **Citymapper:** Available in Vienna, this app helps plan multi-modal journeys combining public transit, walking, and cycling.

- **Google Maps:** Offers accurate navigation, public transport schedules, and walking routes.

- **Car Rental Apps:** Many international car rental agencies offer their own apps for bookings, roadside assistance, and managing rentals.

- **Parkopedia:** Useful for finding parking lots, prices, and availability in cities and towns.

- **Rome2rio:** A global transport planner that provides information on trains, buses, ferries, and flights within Austria.

With these transportation options and tips, you'll be well prepared to enjoy all that Austria has to offer—from vibrant urban culture to stunning natural landscapes—without stress or confusion.

162

Chapter 14
Travel Tips, Safety, and Etiquette

Traveling in Austria offers a rich blend of history, culture, and breathtaking landscapes. To ensure your trip is safe, enjoyable, and respectful of local customs, it's important to be prepared. This chapter covers essential **health and safety guidelines**, key **local customs and etiquette**, **useful German phrases**, important **emergency contacts and services**, and tailored **tips for families, solo travelers, and seniors**. Following these tips will help you navigate Austria confidently and comfortably.

Health and Safety Guidelines

General Health Tips

- **Stay Hydrated:** Austria has excellent tap water quality, so drinking water from the tap is safe and recommended.

- **Sun Protection:** During summer months, especially in alpine regions, the sun can be strong. Use sunscreen, wear hats, and sunglasses.

- **Altitude Awareness:** When traveling in mountainous regions (e.g., Tirol or the Alps), be mindful of altitude sickness symptoms like

163

headaches, dizziness, or nausea. Take it easy and acclimatize slowly.

- **Food Safety:** Austrian food hygiene standards are very high. Enjoy street food and local restaurants without worry, but always check the freshness of dairy and meat products.

- **Vaccinations:** No special vaccinations are required for Austria, but keep routine immunizations up to date, including tetanus and influenza if traveling in winter.

- **Travel Insurance:** Always purchase comprehensive travel insurance that covers health emergencies, accidents, and cancellations.

COVID-19 and Infectious Diseases

- Austria has managed COVID-19 regulations dynamically, so check current guidelines before traveling.

- Masks may still be required in hospitals, public transport, and crowded indoor areas.

- Follow general hygiene practices: wash hands frequently, use hand sanitizer, and avoid close contact if you feel unwell.

Transportation Safety

- Use seat belts in cars and public transport where available.

- Be cautious when cycling or hiking, and always follow local safety signs and guidelines.

- In winter, driving in snowy conditions requires winter tires and possibly chains. Drive slowly and maintain a safe distance.

Personal Safety

- Austria is generally very safe, with low crime rates.

- Keep an eye on personal belongings, especially in crowded tourist areas or on public transport, to prevent pickpocketing.

- Avoid poorly lit or isolated areas at night.

- Use hotel safes or secure lockers for valuables.

- Be cautious when accepting drinks or food from strangers.

Local Customs and Behavior

Understanding local customs will help you connect better with Austrians and avoid unintentional offenses.

165

Greetings and Social Etiquette

- **Greetings:** A firm handshake is the standard greeting in formal and business settings. Among close friends or family, a cheek kiss (usually three alternating kisses) may be common.

- Use polite titles and last names unless invited to use first names.

- Say **"Grüß Gott"** (God greet you) in Southern Austria and Bavaria as a friendly hello.

- When entering homes or shops, a brief **"Hallo"** or **"Guten Tag"** is appreciated.

Politeness and Respect

- Austrians value punctuality; being late is considered rude, especially for appointments or social events.

- Speak softly and avoid loud conversations in public places.

- Respect personal space—stand about an arm's length away when talking.

- Wait for your turn in queues and don't push ahead.

Dining Etiquette

166

- Keep your hands visible and resting on the table during meals, but not elbows.

- Say **"Mahlzeit"** (enjoy your meal) before eating, especially in workplace or communal settings.

- Wait for the host or the eldest person to start eating before you begin.

- It is polite to finish everything on your plate unless you are full.

- Tipping is customary but not mandatory—round up the bill or leave about 5-10% in restaurants.

Public Behavior

- Smoking is banned in most indoor public spaces, including restaurants and bars.

- Austria is environmentally conscious—use recycling bins and avoid littering.

- Respect quiet hours, especially in residential areas (usually 10 pm to 6 am).

Photography Etiquette

- Ask permission before photographing people, especially in rural or religious settings.

167

- Some museums and galleries prohibit photography, so look for signs.

Useful Phrases in German

Although many Austrians speak English, learning basic German phrases will enhance your experience and show respect.

English	German (Austrian)	Pronunciation
Hello / Good day	Grüß Gott / Guten Tag	grooss got / goo-ten tahk
Please	Bitte	bit-tuh
Thank you	Danke	dahn-kuh
Yes	Ja	yah
No	Nein	nine
Excuse me / Sorry	Entschuldigung	ent-shool-dee-goong
Do you speak English?	Sprechen Sie Englisch?	shpre-ken zee eng-lish?
I don't understand	Ich verstehe nicht	ikh fer-shteh-uh nikht

168

Where is...?	Wo ist...?	voh ist...?
How much does it cost?	Wie viel kostet das?	vee feel kostet das?
Bathroom	Toilette	toy-let-tuh
Help!	Hilfe!	hil-fuh!
I need a doctor	Ich brauche einen Arzt	ikh brow-kh-uh eye-nen artst
Cheers!	Prost!	prohst!

Emergency Contacts and Services

Knowing who to contact in an emergency is vital for your safety.

Emergency Service	Phone Number	Description
Police	112 or 133	General emergency and crime
Ambulance / Medical	112 or 144	Emergency medical assistance
Fire Department	122	Fire emergencies

Poison Control Center	+43 1 406 43 43	Help for poisoning or toxic substances
Tourist Police	+43 1 31310 200	Assistance specifically for tourists
Roadside Assistance	120 or +43 1 40 20 200	Help for car breakdowns

Hospitals and Pharmacies

- Pharmacies (**Apotheke**) are widespread and usually open during business hours. Many have emergency services with on-call pharmacists.

- Public hospitals are well-equipped; private hospitals may offer additional services.

- Always carry your travel insurance details and identification.

170

Tips for Families, Solo Travelers, and Seniors

Families

- Austria is very family-friendly with numerous attractions for children, including zoos, playgrounds, and interactive museums.

- Use family or group tickets when available for savings on public transport and attractions.

- Most restaurants and cafes provide high chairs and children's menus.

- When hiking or skiing with children, choose trails and slopes suitable for their age and skill level.

- Keep children close in busy areas and teach them basic safety rules.

Solo Travelers

- Austria is safe and welcoming, with a strong culture of respect and courtesy.

- Stay in well-reviewed accommodations in central or safe neighborhoods.

- Use public transportation, which is reliable and well-monitored.

- Join group tours or activities if you want company or local insights.

- Keep emergency contacts handy and share your itinerary with family or friends.

Seniors

- Austria offers excellent healthcare facilities and accessibility in public transport and attractions.

- Consider renting mobility aids if needed; many tourist offices can provide this service.

- Take advantage of senior discounts offered in many museums, transport services, and attractions.

- Plan rest days between active excursions to avoid fatigue.

- Dress in layers and prepare for sudden weather changes, especially in mountainous areas.

Additional Travel Tips

- **Money:** Austria uses the Euro (€). Credit and debit cards are widely accepted, but carry some cash for small shops or rural areas.

- **Electricity:** Standard European plugs (Type F) with 230V, 50Hz. Bring adapters if your devices use different plugs.

- **Time Zone:** Central European Time (CET), UTC +1; Central European Summer Time (CEST), UTC +2 in summer.

- **Internet:** Free Wi-Fi is common in cafes, hotels, and public spaces. Consider a local SIM card for mobile data.

- **Climate:** Weather varies from mild summers to snowy winters. Pack accordingly.

Being mindful of health and safety guidelines, respecting local customs, knowing key German phrases, and being prepared for emergencies will make your Austrian trip smooth and enjoyable. Whether you're traveling with family, alone, or as a senior, Austria offers a welcoming environment with plenty of support and amenities.

Embrace the culture, stay safe, and enjoy the stunning landscapes, historic cities, and warm hospitality that make Austria a top travel destination!

173

Conclusion
Your Austrian Adventure
Awaits

As you reach the final pages of this travel guide, it's time to reflect on all that Austria has to offer and prepare yourself for an unforgettable journey. From the imperial grandeur of Vienna to the tranquil lakeside charm of Hallstatt, the majestic peaks of the Alps to the vibrant cultural festivals that pulse through every season, Austria promises an experience that captivates every kind of traveler.

Embrace the Spirit of Austria

Austria is a country where centuries-old traditions meet modern sophistication. Its rich history is etched into stunning architecture, majestic palaces, and world-class museums. The cultural heartbeat of the nation is alive through music, art, festivals, and the warm hospitality of its people. Whether you are a history buff, an outdoor enthusiast, a foodie, or an art lover, Austria invites you to explore its many facets.

The cities are alive with energy yet maintain a graceful pace. Vienna's elegant coffee houses, Salzburg's musical heritage, Innsbruck's alpine charm — each city offers unique stories waiting to be discovered. Meanwhile, the

174

idyllic countryside and mountain villages offer peaceful retreats where you can reconnect with nature and yourself.

Planning Your Journey Ahead

Traveling in Austria requires a blend of curiosity, preparation, and openness to new experiences. This guide has equipped you with practical advice on where to go, what to see, and how to navigate the country confidently. You now know how to immerse yourself in Austria's cultural richness, enjoy its culinary delights, and safely explore its diverse landscapes.

Remember to tailor your itinerary to your interests — whether you want a fast-paced city adventure or a slow, scenic retreat in the mountains. Consider visiting during different seasons to experience Austria's ever-changing charm, from winter snow festivals to vibrant summer hikes.

Making the Most of Your Visit

Austria's true magic lies in the little moments: the aroma of fresh pastries in a Viennese bakery, the sound of a Mozart sonata echoing through Salzburg's streets, the breathtaking views from an alpine trail, or the warmth of a local's smile in a mountain inn. Allow yourself to savor these moments without rushing.

Take time to connect with locals, try authentic dishes beyond the usual tourist menus, and participate in traditional festivals and markets. Use the useful phrases provided in this guide to engage meaningfully, showing respect and appreciation for Austrian culture.

Staying Safe and Respectful

No matter where your travels take you in Austria, your safety and respect for local customs are paramount. Always be mindful of the health and safety tips discussed earlier, practice courteous behavior, and remain aware of your surroundings.

Austria's welcoming environment is best experienced when visitors show appreciation for its heritage, natural environment, and community values. Sustainable tourism practices help preserve Austria's beauty for generations to come.

A Country for Every Traveler

Austria caters to all travelers — families will find safe, educational, and fun activities; solo adventurers will discover new friendships and enriching experiences; seniors will enjoy accessible attractions and peaceful landscapes. Adventure seekers can ski, hike, and bike, while culture lovers can immerse themselves in music, art, and history.

No matter your travel style, Austria's diversity ensures you will find your perfect experience.

176

Final Words of Encouragement

Travel is about exploration and discovery, but also about connection — with new places, cultures, and yourself. Austria offers all these opportunities in abundance. Step out of your comfort zone, embrace the unknown, and let Austria surprise you.

Every cobbled street, every mountain trail, every melody and meal is part of a story that you will carry with you long after your trip ends. This journey will enrich your understanding of the world and inspire future travels.

Prepare, Pack, and Go!

With this guide as your companion, you are ready to embark on your Austrian adventure. Prepare your luggage thoughtfully, pack with the seasons in mind, and keep your itinerary flexible to seize spontaneous moments.

Austria's landscapes await your footsteps, its cities invite your exploration, and its people welcome you warmly. Your adventure is not just a trip; it's an experience that will touch your heart, mind, and soul.

So, set your sights on Austria — a land of beauty, culture, and unforgettable experiences. Your Austrian adventure awaits.

Printed in Dunstable, United Kingdom

63623242R00100